"We Shall Come Home Victorious."

Stories of World War II Veterans

HONOR · EDUCATE · PRESERVE
Remembering and Honoring our Veterans

An Honor Project of the

Veterans History Museum of the Carolinas

Brevard, North Carolina

Sixth Edition – May 1, 2020

Stories Collected by Janis Allen

Edited by Elaine Goar and Michael McCarthy

"We Shall Come Home Victorious."

Stories of World War II Veterans

"WE SHALL COME HOME VICTORIOUS."

PERFORMANCE
LEADERSHIP
PUBLICATIONS

Printed in the United States of America by KDP

KDP.com

Cover Design: Advertising PLUS, Lawrenceville, Georgia

adplus@mac.com

This book is for sale on Amazon.com

All proceeds from this book go to the Veterans History Museum of the Carolinas,

Brevard, North Carolina

DEDICATION

This book is dedicated to the World War II Veterans who answered the call of duty.
They saved our nation. They saved Western civilization.
May we honor them by preserving and protecting our constitutional republic
that gives us the blessings of liberty.

At the Patriotic Pops Concert at Brevard Music Center on July 4, 2017, family members of service members were asked to stand up when the anthem of that armed service was played.
This was written for my brothers after our dad passed away at the age of 98.

I Stood Up for Dad

I stood up for Dad
Because he stood up for me.
In war and peace,
He stood and served at sea.

Standing his watches,
With long looks scanning the sea
For dangers to his shipmates.
We all were in his lee.

A sailor fallen overboard,
Disabled ships and yachts
The ever ready Coast Guard
With Dad on ready watch

Semper Paratus, always ready,
He was there to do his part
And he in turn taught his sons
To likewise do our part.

Dad stood up for us,
And is standing still
Behind our shoulders
Casting a tall shadow.

In my shadow
I see his shadow,
And know he is there behind me,
Standing up for us still.

Michael McCarthy, July, 2017

ABOUT THIS BOOK: AN HONOR PROJECT

These are stories of World War II veterans who were born in the Carolinas, moved here and made the Carolinas their homes, or whose daughters and sons live here and share their parents' stories.

It began in 2016 with 17 stories. Now this sixth edition presents a total of 35 stories. With each new person I meet or learn about, I am more in awe of the courageous jobs they did to serve their country and to save the world from tyranny.

Telling their stories is our way of honoring them for what they did for us. That is why we call this an Honor Project.

ABOUT THE TITLE

"We shall come home victorious." These were the words spoken by my daddy, G.E. Allen, on a record he made and mailed to my mother during the war. Above is a picture of that record (his full message is on page 232).

I'm touched each time I hear his voice on that record, sounding confident that we would win the war. These words represent that unselfish and brave generation who saved our civilization.

Daddy predicted right, thank the Lord.

"WE SHALL COME HOME VICTORIOUS."

ACKNOWLEDGMENTS

FOR THE MUSEUM

This book was inspired by the opening of the Western North Carolina Military History Museum (now the Veterans History Museum of the Carolinas) on October 22, 2016. Twelve years of work had been done before that day to collect artifacts, organize exhibits, provide exhibit space, publicize the museum, secure speakers, sweep the floors, and be present during its opening in Brevard, North Carolina. Thank you to Emmett Casciato, Ken Corn, David Morrow, Tom Bugala, Phil Davis, and Mike Domokur.

FOR THE BOOK

I thank you for your help and encouragement.

Mike McCarthy	Elaine Goar
Faye Edney	Michel Robertson
Bill Robertson	Frank Duckworth
Anne Robbins	Kit Lemaire
Joe Lemaire	Angus Graham
Jane Clark	Donna Maag
Greg Maag	Becky Francis Green
Don Tate	Evelyn Brush
John Luzena	Carl Burkhart
David Morrow	Jana Gruber
Ray Norris	

Janis Allen

CONTENTS

ALPHABETICAL LISTING OF NAMES

"WE SHALL COME HOME VICTORIOUS."

"I never had any idea that we wouldn't win. None of us did."

> Ray Pegram
> Radio Operator on a C-47
>
> Dropped the 101st Airborne Pathfinder Paratroops on D-Day

"I would join up again. I would do it for my country."

> Dorothy Schieve, on her 95th birthday, October 25, 2019
>
> U.S. Army WAC
> Served in England and France, WWII

World War II Timeline

World War II was a global war that began September 1, 1939 and ended September 2, 1945. Aggressions began earlier, as listed below.

- 1931: Japan occupies Manchuria.

- 1936: Mussolini conquers Ethiopia.

- 1937: Japan invades China.

- 1938: British Prime Minister Chamberlain lets Hitler take part of Czechoslovakia. Chamberlain calls this appeasement "peace in our time".

- 1939: Hitler annexes all of Czechoslovakia. Hitler and ally Stalin invade Poland. England and France declare war against Germany.

- 1940: British and French armies evacuated at Dunkirk. Hitler controls most of Europe. Italy joins the Axis powers, Germany and Japan.

- July-October 1940: The Battle of Britain. Hitler bombs Britain nightly.

- March 1941: U.S. begins lend-lease program to Great Britain.

- June 1941: Hitler invades "ally" Russia. U.S. begins lend-lease to Russia.

- December 7, 1941: Japan bombs Pearl Harbor. U.S. declares war on Japan and Germany. Great Britain, France and the U.S. became the "Allies".

- 1942: Hitler begins round-up and genocide of six million Jews.

- 1942-43: U.S. fights naval battles in the Pacific against Japan.

- 1943: The Allies win North Africa, then invade Sicily and Italy.

- 1944: The Allies invade Europe on the beaches of Normandy, France.

- May 7, 1945: Germany surrenders. The war ends in Europe.

- August 1945: The U.S. drops atomic bombs on Hiroshima and Nagasaki. Japan surrenders September 2, 1945, ending the war in the Pacific.

"WE SHALL COME HOME VICTORIOUS."

THE WAR IN EUROPE AND NORTH AFRICA

FOLLOWING ARE THE PERSONAL STORIES
OF VETERANS
WHO SERVED IN EUROPE AND NORTH AFRICA.

"WE SHALL COME HOME VICTORIOUS."

Tom McCrary, U.S. Army

Infantryman Tom McCrary, when he enlisted in the U.S. Army in 1943

Tom McCrary was born in 1926 in Transylvania County, North Carolina.
He was drafted into the U.S. Army in 1943 and served in the 86th Black Hawk Infantry Division.
He served in both Europe and in the Pacific. He was discharged in 1946.

Basic Training at Camp Blanding, Florida

In 1943, eighteen-year-old Tom McCrary lived in Little River, now known as Crab Creek Road. He entered the Army at Fort Bragg, North Carolina. He was sent to Camp Blanding, Florida, for 18 weeks of basic training. His unit was getting ready to ship out to the Pacific when they were redirected to Europe to back up General Patton in the Battle of the Bulge.

Tom recalled, "I went to Fort Jackson [in Columbia, South Carolina]. That's where I started off, but of course I went to Fort Bragg to be inducted. That was 1943. Of course I was drafted. When you became 18 in 'them thar days,' you got the little card that classified you. My dad was in the well-drilling business, which is the business I retired from.

"He was drilling wells then. My dad was in World War I. I became 18 and got my card, and my Dad said that the work was essential. Back then, if the work was considered essential you could get a deferment. He repaired the pumping systems in two or three counties, and he said, 'I've got to have you; I'm out of men.' My Dad said he could get me a deferment, but I said no, no I'm going on.

"I was in the infantry, Army, 86th Infantry Division. They called it the Blackhawk. Like I say, when I lost that cedar chest . . . [It was stolen from his home.] with my uniform from the war, I lost other mementos of the war as well. Of course I couldn't get into it [his uniform] now no way. They shipped me out to Camp Blanding. That's in the northern end of Florida. I spent 18 weeks there training."

Tom recalled an incident from basic training in Camp Blanding, Florida: "We stayed out two weeks on bivouac with those mosquitoes down there. We start back home. You get a ten-day leave. But if you don't make it, you're going to have to stay another day. And it was a 25-mile hike. That was the first one I'd ever been on. I had a real good buddy. He was married and had two kids. We were struggling along. Once in a while the column would slow down, but then we'd have to run. I was 18 years old then. I'm a heap of man.

"We'd have to stop every 15 miles, I think, and change socks. A medic would come by and look at your feet. And take that little break. He'd always hit my feet and say, 'You're alright.' A lot of those soldiers' feet would swell. My old buddy there, he [was struggling]. His heel was bleeding. I tried to get him to fall out, but he said his wife was coming down to Jacksonville. So I took his gun. I was young. He was in his thirties. That was old.

"The lieutenant that trained us, he came running up to find me. He was part of the training cadre. He would train another bunch every eighteen weeks. He had two rifles on each shoulder. And he told me, 'Is that all you can do, Mac? Can't you help somebody else? You sissy!' The butts of those rifles were bumping him. What I didn't know then, see, he did that year in and year out. He was tough but that was my first, and I was dying. When I got back with that old sulphur water I laid down in that trough and drunk a gallon and blowed up. I didn't come home that week!"

Amphibious Training in California

"Then I was shipped out to California. Camp Callen. I was in three camps out there: Camp Callen, Camp Cook, and Camp St. Luis Obispo, they called it. We trained near the Marines. I thought I wanted to be a Marine.

"I didn't know it, but I was color-blind. Back in the 30s and 40s, colors didn't mean a heck of a lot. I thought growing up maybe I was just a little slow learning colors. But they said, 'You're color-blind. You can't get in the Marines. You can't get anywhere but the Army.' But they had 500 shipped out of Bragg [and I was held back]. In those days they didn't tell you anything. I ended up in a barracks with five or six men that were going into the Army. We came to the conclusion we were all color-blind.

"We trained right next to the Marines. Trained to land on beaches off LCIs, which were Landing Craft Infantry. We were getting ready to ship out. We were going to the Pacific, of course. We had tropical gear, we had jungle boots, we had mosquito nets, and they gave you 20 shots [inoculations], you know, to prevent diseases.

"I was in California doing basic training as a replacement. A replacement in the Army, in WWII, you got the crap of everything. They'd give you every detail they could. Well, I joined this outfit that had been over in Germany and got shot up bad. Took a lot of casualties. So they sent them home. What was left of them. To recuperate. Well, every one of them they'd give a sergeant stripe if they'd been over there and done a little fighting. I joined that crowd, and it was miserable [for a private like me].

"My problem was, they put me in a rifle company. I was shooting over their heads with a machine gun day in and day out [as part of infantry training]. They give you an MOS [military occupational specialty] number. My MOS number called for mortar man, and not rifleman. It came on the bulletin board that anybody had MOS number so and so, go down to headquarters. And I thought, I'm not liking this much where I'm at now, where they are all superior to me and I take the brunt of all the problems. So I go down there and they line me up to go out with a mortar, on a Saturday evening, with these two lieutenants.

"They took four of us out there and wanted to see if we knew anything about a mortar. Parked on a hill. These two lieutenants wanted to be off on the Saturday and wanted to get back. Had a case of beer, drinking it. Parked down the hill was an old German tank. This was in California. They was practicing shooting at it. They let each one of us set that thing [the mortar] and shoot it. I just knew I'd screw up, but I didn't. Did pretty good. So that put me in to this mortar squad.

"I told one of my buddies, 'I'm going to be carrying a 45 [automatic pistol]. That's all I'm going to be carrying.' That was a bunch of bull, of course. He was kidding me about not having to carry that M1, that 9 lb. rifle. But now I had to carry a 45 pound base plate for a mortar."

Reinforcements for The Battle of the Bulge

"All of a sudden, they jerked us up and we went to New York. We went to Europe. It was the time of the [Battle of] the Bulge. I reckon Patton needed some more men over there. So I ended up in France. Le Havre, France. I'll never forget that name. Little seaport town, and it's about an inch and a half of snow on the ground and the wind blowing.

"When we got off that ship, we had khaki pants, khaki shirt, mosquito net that was in our pack. That's all we had to go on. They shipped us out in a hurry. They needed men on the line bad. But we didn't have any dang [warm] clothes! Their story was that a sub got our supply ship. We finally got something to wear. We were sleeping on the ground, and we found that you could put that mosquito net on the ground and that would help it insulate for warmth. It was winter time and the French looked at us like we were crazy. We had little field jackets. Then they shuttled us out, scattered us out.

Tom McCrary with his map of the routes taken by the Blackhawk Division, 86th Infantry, during World War II

"The story was, in that little town of Le Havre, a private in the service, you know, doesn't find out much. I was told you can't go outside. You can't go by yourself. You have to have a loaded gun when you go outside; the French don't like us. And the story was somebody in Intelligence goofed up and the Germans knew when we were coming. They [the Germans] pulled back and shoved all the civilians up there into the little city, and that's why the French were bitter. They [the Germans] killed most of them and flattened that little town. So that's the reason we couldn't get along with the French. They were real bitter.

"So then I ended up going through Germany and ended up in Austria, where I spent most of my time. We hooked up with the 24th Infantry Division. I remember they had a rainbow on their shirtsleeve. They switched us off on the front lines. I'll never forget seeing these guys. See, we were fresh. They looked at us like we were like Boy Scouts, we still had asphalt on our feet. But those seasoned soldiers looked down on us, and really, [when] we started on the line, a private could give you orders over a lieutenant, you know. An old seasoned soldier would tell us what to do. I remember feeling that they were looking at us and saying, 'Why, a bunch of kids over here,' you know. They were really seasoned, all of them with a beard and dirty and all that.

"I was part of a mortar squad. It was called an 81 millimeter mortar. I carried the tube. Then I carried the base plate, the bottom of it. That made me the third gunner. So if the first one [gunner] got killed, and the second one got killed, I'd come in [to operate the mortar]. A mortar squad would have three men, plus back-up people, carrying the ammunition. I had to carry 3 or 4 rounds, plus the 45 lb. base plate. We had a jeep most of the time. You couldn't carry that plate [long distances]." [The jeep would transport the mortar as far as possible, and then Pfc. Tom McCrary would carry the base plate and 4 shells to the spot where the mortar would be set up to fire.]

Spotter says "Direct Hit!"

"When we first hit the lines [in Europe] I was of course green. Kind of had a slip-up. Germans drove through the line and was coming toward us pretty rapid. They were shooting artillery over our heads. I mean, it wasn't fifty feet up there [overhead], and I knew this was the real thing. Well, I was a second gunner on a mortar, 81mm mortar. I carried what they called the base plate. I could take that thing and hook it in my belt. It was cast aluminum. It weighed 45 pounds. Well, I could run with that thing, day in and day out, in practice, and carry four 11-pound shells on my belt.

"I could run with that thing, believe it or not. You had your backpack. Of course there wasn't too much in that. You wouldn't run a long ways to go set up a gun.

"Anyways, we were on top of a pretty hill. I never will forget it. All at once, coming over the radio, this that and the other, and the lieutenants excited too, they weren't experienced. So my job was to take that base plate, which I'd done a hundred times, and I'd pitch it, and with two feet stomp it down with the lugs on it. Well, all the excitement and the cursing and the hollering, get this and get that, another mortar was sitting right over by me there.

"I stomped that base plate in and grabbed the shell, and that base plate went out from under that thing and the tube laid down. It was a wonder we hadn't killed one of our own men, you know. Well, that really rattled us up. What happened, when I stomped that thing down, there was a root or something under it, and I didn't get it seated right.

"That really tore up the bunch [of us]. We were scared, scared and here comes all the artillery over. We go back and set it up again. Lo and behold, we hit a limb. That changed where it went. [The shell ricocheted off the limb.] The limb was no bigger than 3 inches. This lieutenant, he went haywire then.

"Now we are in trouble sure enough. They are coming at us and we can't even get a round off. Mortar next to us was plunking shells. Pum, pum. So we were complete failures. Well, the next round, our spotter was talking back to us. The one that hit the tree, it glanced off. The spotter said he couldn't see it. The next time, the third time, we just guessed at it. He called back in and said it was a direct hit. He called for eleven rounds. Well that emptied everything we had. So, he said we had really fixed that up. There was a little squad of Germans with a couple of trucks and a side car motorcycle.

"That night, we laid back. We weren't moving forward. [We were in] an old blown out building. Someone come around and said, 'The colonel wants to talk to squad eleven.' Well we looked at each other and said, 'Ooh, we are going to get a talking now.' The colonel came round and shook hands with all of us. I never did forget what he said. He said, 'Now men, this is what wins the damn war. It takes men just like you to do it and you done it. And I want to congratulate you.' See, he didn't know about [the goof up]. Someone said, 'You reckon we'll get the Purple Heart?' I said, 'No!' But he complemented us. We had just screwed up bad.

"The spotter had told us, you got a direct hit. I fed that thing, pum, pum, pum. The same charge. You put charges in it for the distance. And I remember I was shaking all over getting those charges and getting them right. You put two extra in and you go a little farther. So that was my heroic stand there. That certified me as an infantryman, I guess."

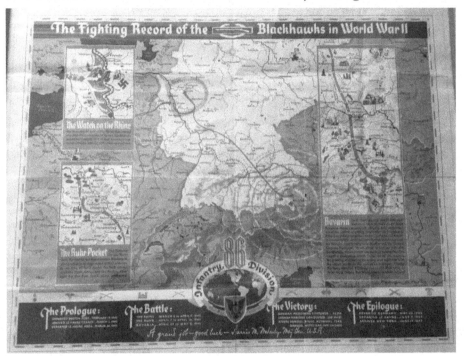

**Map of the routes taken and battles fought by the Blackhawk Division,
86th Infantry during World War II**

When a Jeep Trailer Pinned My Leg

"I turned over in a jeep one time. A trailer pulled by a jeep. A shell hit right in front of the jeep and it went down in the shell hole. Well, the first thing I knew I was on the ground. I was half asleep from swinging on that jeep for a day or two, and I hit the ground and one leg was under the trailer. There was about five of us hanging on it, and they all got off; it slung them off. And I know I was laying there, snow was on the ground. I kidded a buddy, a buddy from Missouri. We had an old jug of lard shortening and we'd stop and cook in the little towns. Fry taters, that was all we could do. They had taters everywhere, you know. So I always kidded him, I was hollering at Bob, saying, 'Bob, get me out of here!' He didn't really realize I was under that thing. So they picked it up, and of course 'Medic! Medic! Medic!'

"So I'll never forget the medic started in right here with his knife and cut my OD [government issue] pants right down to my leg, and there sat my bottom in the snow. And he kept telling me, 'Mac (Everybody called me Mac.), Mac, you ain't going to die. What are you afraid of? What you scared of?' [I was shaking.] I tried to explain to him if he put his tail down there in that snow he'd need to keep from shaking [too].

"But my leg was just bruised. I really thought it was broken. 'Course they tied a carbine (short rifle) around the leg and the first thing I knew they left me alone, nobody around but an old woman and an old man in a house. No communication, and they were trying to make me comfortable up next to the fireplace. I was getting leery. [My unit] went on. They had picked up a lot of fire there and they just left me. Well, they started with me to the ambulance, and they decided I wasn't as bad hurt as somebody else, so they didn't have room [for me]. So they just left me with these people.

"Sometime during the night I got up. I could walk with a walking stick. It was out in the country. I walked up to the road. I seen these two cat-eyes coming. That's what they called them on those jeeps so you couldn't see them from overhead, the little headlights. I knew that was one of ours. It was two lieutenants, and they said, 'Soldier, what are you doing here?' And I said, 'Well, they went on and left me.' One asked, 'Left you?' And I said, 'Hell, they were drawing a lot of fire there, they couldn't stay with me.' And they said, 'Where is your outfit?' and I said, 'They went that way is all I know.'

"They ended up getting on the radio and finding out where my outfit was. They had moved on and made it on over a mile away. They gave me a ride [to where my outfit was] and I went on into this old building that was blown all to pieces, sides out of it and all. It was snowing then. There wasn't a place to lay down nowhere. Everybody was on the floor of course. Everybody was dead tired. We'd been going a few days. I finally got a place out at the end of the hall. There was a draft, and I had a miserable night.

"But got in line the next morning. It shaped up, the sun was shining. I guess there was fifty of us. There was a line for those of us with an injury, and I got in that line. I thought, 'My leg isn't hurt,' so I fell out of that line. So that was the only scratch I got."

Beer in Berchtesgaden

"So I ended up going through France, and then Germany, and then Austria, and then Belgium. When the war was over I had just left Switzerland. We went up to Hitler's Berchtesgaden. When I go up on the mountain here, Pisgah Forest, it never fails. I wind up going toward the [Blue Ridge] Parkway, my mind goes back, this is like Hitler's hideout up there. I went downstairs in that Berchtesgaden and the concrete was five feet thick. They came in and bombed the hound out of that, but they missed him. Our story was, missed Hitler by a day.

"So we were down at the bottom of that thing and they had barrels with brass handles on them with beer. So we were fighting over the beer and they wouldn't let us drink it until they

ran a test on it to make sure it wasn't poisoned. So I got my canteen cup and got in line, and then these French soldiers came and we didn't get along good with them. They claimed they were the ones took it [conquered it], and we said we took this place.

Left: Berchtesgaden (Hitler's hideout) before the British bombed it in 1945. (stock photo)

"That's where I ended up in Europe. I headed back to Le Havre, France where I landed. As the war wound down, it's really hard to believe, but we were out in a rural area of Belgium, and the people didn't think the war was over. The Air Force flew over and dropped these little pamphlets, telling the Belgian people that the war was over. They really didn't know. They were loyal and faithful to Hitler. These little silver strips of paper flooded the country and the little towns. We'd go on and the war was over, peace was signed, but they were still blowing up bridges ahead of us. I just thought, what a shame. They wouldn't accept the fact.

"Come back to Le Havre and got on a boat. Well, we got out in the water [the sea] and talk was, 'We're going to Japan.' And others said, 'No, we aren't going to Japan.'"

Germans in Transylvania County?

"While I was on my ten days leave here at home, a crop-duster dove over the house to spray the field next to my Dad's house where they grew beans. I like to hit the floor! Then it was kind of funny, I looked outside at the fields and there was about fifty German soldiers. They still had their blue-looking uniforms on. They were using them to gather these beans. So I eased down to the road there. I had my khakis on. Their interpreter get ahold of me and asked, 'Where did you go? What did you do?' [They wanted news of their homeland.] It was hard to believe that we'd come home and they were still holding those German soldiers there. Right near my front door, where I used to play throwing clods of dirt."

Preparing for the Invasion of Japan

"But I got back to California and they ran us through a course or two, refresher course. That was really what we had trained for [originally]—that amphib training, when they rushed us over to help old Patton out.

"We [the Blackhawk Division] got credit for a lot of things [in our European theatre of operations] like the number of prisoners we captured. We were attached to Patton's 3rd Army. What we were doing mostly, because we were considered green, was holding. They put us on the line to hold [against the German advance at the Battle of the Bulge]. They pushed us back and then we wouldn't let them cross the Rhine river. They told us when we went over that they would use us to cross the rivers [because we were amphib], but they didn't. Patton mostly used us to hold against the big [German] surges.

"That was how they would break us in [with an assignment to hold the line against a German advance]. So I came back and headed overseas [from California]. On the deck of the ship they had an area marked off by chalk and every day we would have an orientation. It would say our position was to go into Tokyo Bay. It would show where our battalion would go. I remember distinctly they said we'd be in the 11th wave. They'd have Rangers and technical people in there and mark on the deck in chalk. We'd study that daily.

"Of course, when we were training in California, we'd go out (they said) about 100 miles. They'd bombard an island and then we'd simulate taking it. We'd practice going down the rope ladders. There would be 24 men doing a 'dry run' they called it. They would send planes in and put smoke down and drop paratroopers. You know, we were trained for that kind of warfare more than the type we did in Germany.

14

"Between Luzon [The Philippines] and Japan, they said it was about 800 miles. I guess there were 40 vessels, cruisers and destroyers and aircraft carriers in the formation going over there. It was something else to see.

"Word came out on the ship that Truman dropped that bomb. Said we were going back to California. And everybody was real excited. That was one day and the next day I was out on deck and the fleet was not with us. There were just a few ships. The war was over.

"So they backed us up and said we needed to do a little cleaning up on Luzon (That's the biggest island in the Philippines.) They had bypassed a lot of Japs. The story was they were in the mountains. There were tales that they were cannibals. I got rid of my gun and got to driving a truck, a supply truck back toward Manila, which was about 60 miles on a rough road. A time or two a truck would be hijacked. The Japanese soldiers in the mountains would come out. They had caves [to hide in]. The war was over, but every day or two we'd lose somebody. They wanted food. They would kill the driver and take what he had on the truck. They'd hide out back in the hills. They always kidded me that they were cannibals. My buddies would say, 'Tom, if they get you those big white legs of yours—they'd enjoy you!' I thought that was a hell of a way to talk to a man!

"After six months they wised up and stopped sending out American soldiers and put Filipinos in [the trucks]. We were told we'd be there a year at the most, and then we'd be going back to California. Well it ended up I was over there 18 months [on the island of Luzon]. Claimed they didn't have any shipping to take us out. Of course the harbor I know was full of wrecked ships, but they got us in. So they wanted to keep us over there just to ride shotgun [on the supply trucks]. We had a machine gun on the back of a Deuce and a Half, we called it, and we patrolled the roads and looked for traces of the Japanese soldiers.

"They said we needed more shots [inoculations] before we could come back home. A couple of times we got ready to go, packed up what little we had, and found the ship was fully loaded. They'd say, 'Go back home. You can catch the next one.' That was really depressing. I was there eighteen dad-blamed months after the end of the war.

"About halfway through those eighteen months I ran into a friend of mine. I was with him in Europe. I hadn't seen him. He was raised [promoted] on the field over in Europe. I kidded him about it a lot. They gave him those gold bars. He did a 'York deal' [Sergeant York was a hero in WWI who single handedly captured dozens of German soldiers.] and slipped around a hill and did something extraordinary. He had been my Sergeant. So he was raised [promoted to 2nd Lieutenant] in the field. He was a pretty sharp dude anyway.

15

"I ran into him while I was driving that truck. He says, 'What's going on, Mac? What are you doing?' I said, 'Driving into Manila. Dusty roads. No windshield.' He said, 'I'll tell you what to do. I'm over a kind of rest area down on the end of the island.' It was where the soldiers could go and stay a week every six months. He was in charge of it. He said, 'Why don't you come down and help me?' I said, 'Aww they won't let me out of the motor pool.' He said, 'I'll tell you what I'll do. I'll have it on your bulletin board that we need volunteers.' Well, you know that you don't volunteer in the Army. If you do, you'll be rolling concrete or something [unpleasant]. Nobody volunteers, but he said, 'You volunteer.'

"I volunteered and they called me down to headquarters and he transferred me off down there. All he wanted me to do, he told me, 'You just keep your eyes open and let me know what's going on. If we got any trouble you can tell me.' I never did forget, he came to me one time and said, 'Tom I need some help.' Him a lieutenant and me a little old private. And he said, 'Some damn body put a goat in my tent. It chewed everything I got, my fancy dress uniform and everything.' He said, 'Now you listen, you go down to the bar and you be with them boys and you find out who did it. Now I helped you out, so you help me out.' Silly things like that. I tried, but I never did find out who did it.

"So the last four or five months I had in the service I had it made. I had a jeep, and I had nothing to do but go check on this and that. That was the only real good break I got.

"So finally I crossed back over that pond. Seemed like everybody else was home. I'd write home and they'd say, 'So and so is out.' I'd think, he went in the Army after I did! We were froze over there [in Luzon]. So I went home. They said, 'Do you want to volunteer [to reenlist] and I said, 'No, I'm going home.' I spent less than three years in both the Pacific and the Atlantic [European theatre of war]. Moved around a lot and had a chance of being in a lot of real rough skirmishes. In Europe it was pretty rough, but nothing compared to the soldiers who had been over there for years before I got there. By the time I got over there, that Bulge had stopped. It was beginning to be over.

"That was a boo-boo, to send a whole division over there, it looked like to me. They always said Patton demanded more men. Course, I never did see Mr. Patton, I never did see MacArthur. I was doing KP, I guess."

Return to Transylvania County

"When I returned from the Pacific, they sent me to Fort Bragg. I got out of the Army and came home to Transylvania County. My dad was a well driller and I went back to work for him. I wanted to do something else, but he had lost some of his men and he needed me.

"When I was in Luzon at the recreation area, many weekends when the others were drinking beer I would get in the habit of going out there and parking my truck and getting on the cranes and bulldozers and just play. They were just sitting there rusting down. I thought, now this is my gift and that when I returned home I would go into the grading business. I would get a GI loan.

"But I worked with my dad. When he passed away, I just stuck with well drilling. He had old equipment and he wouldn't get anything modern. Of course here I come, this young spurt telling him what he ought to do. I'm sure that didn't go over good. I kept on and on. I finally threatened him, 'Well I'm going to quit.' He said, 'You have never been hungry since you set down at my table.' I talked him into buying some light equipment, new equipment. He made me go half and half with him. We did pretty good. We bought two or three of those little machines. I was the superintendent with three crews going.

"My dad died in 1957. I had a friend down in South Carolina who was a big water well equipment distributor. He helped me get a loan for $100,000 from a bank in Spartanburg, and I bought a big well drilling rig. This was in the 1960s. That much debt made me nervous. I'm old fashioned and believe in paying my debts. I retired in 1995. My stepson took over the business. I said, 'I'm done. I've had dirt in my hair, my ears.' I've been so fortunate. I had good help. Some men stayed with me for 20-25 years.

"In 1943 I was living a mile from where I'm living at the present, which was Little River. It's now called Crab Creek Road, where my wife, Jayne, and I live. I only moved a mile and a half in my 90 years. So I'm truly a native all right."

Since retiring, Tom's hobby is welding.

Tom McCrary in 2016

"WE SHALL COME HOME VICTORIOUS."

Lt. Howard Hamilton, U.S. Army Air Corps

Howard Hamilton, a bombardier on B-17 "Flying Fortress" served in the U.S. Army Air Corps 1942-1945. In missions were bombing German rail lines and munitions installations, he was gravely injured when his plane was shot down and held in a German prison camp for 18 months.

Howard Hamilton, father of Brevard veteran LTC Jana Gruber, USAR, Ret, was born October 28, 1923 in the small town of Augusta, KS. Upon graduating from high school in 1942, he joined the Army and became a bombardier on B-17 "Flying Fortress," stationed at Thorpe Abbots, England.

By 1943, a critical stage in WWII, the United States began a high-risk program of strategic daylight bombing of German rail lines and munitions installations. In October 1943, the American strategy had to be altered because of the deadly capable Luftwaffe over German airspace and because the rail lines and munitions installations were being rebuilt at an alarmingly efficient rate.

On Sunday, October 10th the targets changed to actual Germans, their homes, their churches, and the magnificent medieval city of Munster. What resulted over the skies of western Germany was the most vicious sustained carnage of the air war.

In the photo above, Hamilton is kneeling, second from right.

Lt Hamilton was the bombardier in the B-17 they named "Mademoiselle Zig Zag", the lead plane in that particular formation of the 100th Bomb Group (nicknamed The Bloody

100th). As per the usual procedure, the bombardier took control of the aircraft from the pilot just before the bombs were released, making the necessary course adjustments to hit the targets.

There were P-47 fighter escorts several thousand feet above the B-17's, but they were occupied by their own Luftwaffe attack. Hamilton's plane took several hard hits. A 20-millimeter German canon shell ripped through the back of his flak suit, knocking him flat on his face in the nose compartment, his right shoulder broken, his right lung punctured, and both hands bleeding.

One other crewman was dead, and several others wounded. Mlle Zig Zag began to fall out of the sky. The co-pilot motioned for Hamilton to bail out, but he didn't have the strength in his right hand to open the nose compartment door.

He decided the only way was to stand on the door and try to open it with his left hand. The door opened, but his parachute strap, dangling loose over his injured right shoulder, caught on the door handle, leaving him dangling from the plane inches from the propeller with German fighter planes circling and firing repeatedly.

One of the men going out another door came back to see if he had made it out. After much struggle, he freed Hamilton and both parachuted out of the tumbling, fiery wreck of a plane. He was captured dangling from a tree in Germany and taken to a military hospital in Munster.

A lone surgeon worked round the clock on civilians injured by the bombing of the few B-17s that had made it to the targets. Exhausted and out of anesthesia the doctor was not inclined to treat the American fliers who had caused this horror.

Willie Wahle (on the right in this 1992 photo with Howard Hamilton), a German officer who had been wounded at Stalingrad was in charge of the prisoners.

He imagined his fellow German airmen captured over England, and the treatment they would hopefully receive by English physicians. He persuaded the surgeon to operate.

Gerry Karr Hamilton, Howard's wife, knew he was shot down but there was no word on his fate.

In November 1943 Hamilton and his fellow POWs were taken to a camp near Barth on the Baltic shore. In April 1945 the camp was liberated by Russian Cossacks. Eventually they were airlifted by B-17s, and within a few months he arrived home to his wife, Gerry.

While in the POW camp, Lt Hamilton decided to fight the boredom and to "make something of himself." He read history and literature voraciously. He eventually went on to obtain a bachelor, masters and PhD in Electrical Engineering and became chairman of the Electrical Engineering Department at the University of Pittsburgh when he retired.

Below: the Pittsburgh Post-Gazette's May 21, 2000 magazine published the story of the Munster Raid

The caption for the photo (below) in the magazine article read:

B-17s from the 390th Bomb Group turn back toward England after a raid on Marienburg, Germany on October 10, 1943. Planes from the 390th, the 95th, and the 100th made up the ill-fated Munster raid.

Bombardier Howard Hamilton, who was shot down and held as a prisoner of war for almost two years, became head of the Electrical Engineering Department at the University of Pittsburgh.

Hamilton stayed in the Army Reserves, retiring as a Colonel. He passed away in November 1998 and is buried at Arlington National Cemetery.

At right, Howard Hamilton in 1998

A most interesting recounting of the Munster Raid and others during the so-called "black week" can be found in the book THE MUNSTER RAID: BEFORE AND AFTER by Ian L. Hawkins (pictured here).

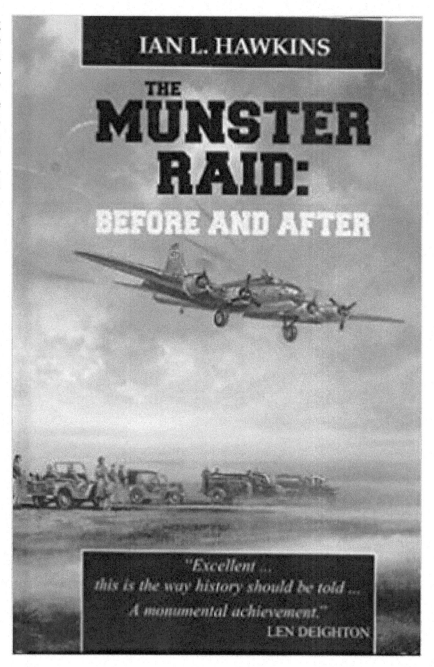

IAN L. HAWKINS

THE MUNSTER RAID: BEFORE AND AFTER

*"Excellent ...
this is the way history should be told ...
A monumental achievement."*
LEN DEIGHTON

Geraldine "Gerry" Hamilton on the Home Front

Gerry Hamilton's story below is adapted from an article in the Pittsburgh Post-Gazette (May 21, 2000) about her and her husband's capture.

Romance and Marriage During Wartime

They'd been married only three months when Howard Hamilton left. They'd known each other only two weeks before they were married.

Gerry Karr (pictured at right), orphaned at 6 and raised with three sisters in a Sioux City orphanage, worked at the Army base where Howard was training in 1943.

"It was not like meeting some stranger in a bar," she said. *"I had all those guys in his outfit to tell me about 'Ham.'*

"You can't live together in close quarters, fly together, eat and drink together without betraying your real self-good or bad. They all told me what a good guy he was. It was probably partly at their urging that he got the idea to ask me to marry him."

It had taken only a few dates. Breakneck romance was not uncommon at the time. The war was on, white hot. Lives were building, solidifying, crystallizing and shattering minute by minute A friend of Gerry's knew a justice of the peace across the state line in Nebraska. They took a taxi.

"The taxi driver," she said, her eyes again lit with happiness, *"he was a witness!"*

Waiting and Wondering

For nearly three months after the raid on Munster, she would know not whether her new husband was dead or alive. The Bloody 100ᵗʰ had been virtually wiped out. Of the 13 Flying Fortresses that had taken off that morning from the airfield at Thorpe Abbots, England, only one returned.

"The hardest part was waiting for my letter saying he'd been killed," she said.

"I used to go roller-skating once or twice a week by myself. I'd think about him, that maybe he'd escaped. The guy who ran the place knew someone was looking for two girls to fill out a six-girl skating act with the Barnum & Bailey Circus. At first, I'd say, 'No, my husband will be home in a month or so.' But then when I didn't hear anything and I didn't get my letter, I decided it might not be such a bad idea to go.

"It was the lure of the circus. You would ride and sleep on the trains. The circus was hard work. A lot of shows every day. We opened in Baltimore, in a theater."

The Telegram

And from her sister, a telegram:

AN INTERCEPTED SHORT-WAVE BROADCAST ORIGINATING IN GERMANY MENTIONED THE NAME OF 1ST LT HOWARD HAMILTON AS A PRISONER OF WAR STOP NO PERSONAL MESSAGE WAS INCLUDED STOP.

"I wrote to him almost every day, but he was only allowed to write once a month or so," she said.

"Many of his letters were about food, the lack of it (900 calories a day). The biggest change seemed to show in these letters from POW camp. The near-death experience intensified his determination to go to college and make his mark on the world, to be good at what he set out to do, to have a secure family life, and to be a good husband to me. He would tell me repeatedly how much he loved me and missed me.

"I prayed a lot – for Howard's safety, for his survival, and eventually for him not to be too changed by what he's gone through."

Returning Home

[In April, 1945 the camp was liberated by Russian Cossacks. Eventually they were airlifted by B-17s, and within a few months he arrived home to his wife, Gerry.]

Howard and Gerry are pictured at right.

Gerry said she awoke one night after the war in a Miami hotel room and found the bombardier standing atop a chest of drawers.

"He was talking about 'holding Hitler at the Verdigris' – which is a river in Kansas.:" she said.

"He had many nightmares that first year of so after he returned. I was nearly stomped to death a couple of times while he crawled over me to get to or away from some imagined danger.

"These incidents lessened and disappeared entirely with about 10 years."

Gerry Hamilton raised four children, three sons and a daughter.

In the mid 1970's Gerry became one of the first paralegals in Pittsburgh. In 1986, at the age of 63, she earned a degree from the University of Pittsburgh.

At right, Gerry is pictured holding a photo made in 2000 of herself and two friends during the war.

Gerry and her daughter Jana are pictured at right.

Gerry died on December 27th, 2016 at age 94.

The Hamiltons' daughter, Jana Gruber, joined the Army Nurse Corps in 1975. At right, she is shown during a cold-weather exercise.

After nine years on active duty, she transferred to the Army Reserves to start a family.

At right, Jana and Mike are shown with their son, Jose Luis, adopted in 1986 when he was 4 years old. He was an orphan in Bolivia and we traveled there to pick him up. He is now 38 years old, married, with two kids, living in Augusta, Georgia.

31

During Desert Shield/Desert Storm, Jana was activated and deployed to Riyadh, Saudi Arabia to work at the King Fahad National Guard Hospital. LTC Gruber retired in 1999. Jana Gruber went on to become a Family Nurse Practitioner in Edgefield, SC. Her husband, Mike Gruber, was Army LTC, retiring after 20 years active duty. They retired to Brevard, NC in 2018.

Jana added, "I feel my father's legacy so often. My memories of him are of a strong, honest, compassionate person. He always told me how proud he was of me. I had the privilege of caring for my mother in her final years. She could only be described as 'quite a character' who would do whatever she could to help another person.

"Thinking of my parents with nostalgia only reminds me of the courage, strength and perseverance of so many of their generation, "the greatest generation."

James P. Morrow, U.S. Army

Lt. James P. Morrow, 551st AAA Battalion

Jim Morrow served in the U.S. Army from 1941 to 1945. He served as a Lab Technician with a Medical Detachment. After OCS he was assigned to the 551st AAA Battalion as Second Lt. and went to Normandy in late July 1944, following Patton across Europe.

By David Morrow, son of James P. Morrow

Just imagine. You are James P. Morrow in 1940. You are 28 years old working at Ecusta in the water treatment plant and farming on the side—growing gladiolus plants and shipping cut flowers to wholesalers.

You get these in the mail:

NOTICE OF CLASSIFICATION

NOTE: Appeal from a classification by a Local Board or Board of Appeal must be made within five days from the date of this notice at the office of the Local Board.

BE ALERT

The person named herein whose Order No. is _19_

Has been classified by Local Board ☒ / Board of Appeals ☐

In Class _I-A_ until _____

_O. H. O__ (Member of Local Board)

Notify your employer of this classification

Nov 15 - 1940 (Date)

This card may be cut on dotted line for convenience in carrying.

Keep in touch with your Local Board

Notify it of any change of address

Notify it of any fact which might change your classification

Failure to notify the Board of these facts within five days of the happening thereof is an Act punishable by fine and imprisonment.

LOCAL BOARD NUMBER 1

BREVARD, TRANSYLVANIA COUNTY, NORTH CAROLINA

March 28, 1941 (Date)

NOTICE OF SELECTION

To: Mr. James Paul Morrow , Order No. 19

You have been selected for training and service under the Selective Training and Service Act of 1940.

You will receive an Order to Report for Induction—such induction to take place on or about April 7, 19 41, when adequate facilities are expected to be available.

This notice is given you in advance for your convenience, and is not an order to report. Persons reporting to the induction station in some instances may be rejected for physical or other reasons. It is well to keep this in mind in arranging your affairs, to prevent any undue hardship if you are rejected at the induction station. If you are employed, you should advise your employer of this notice and of the possibility that you may not be accepted at the induction station. Your employer can then be prepared to replace you if you are accepted, or to continue your employment if you are rejected. The Order to Report for Induction will specify a definite time and place for you to report.

Member of Local Board.

D. S. S. Form 148

On April 8th, 1941, Jim is inducted and becomes a Spec. Sargent by September 24th, 1942.

Working in the Tech-Medical Detachment in Ft. Bragg, N.C., part of his job was to give shots to the recruits. The lab workers made bets on how many of the recruits would faint during the process.

I imagine they were all standing in line in their underwear watching the person in front getting several shots. The lab worker would then pull out a large horse syringe and hold it up so they all could see it. I am sure everyone who was still standing had a good laugh.

The Normandy Invasion and Pushing Toward Germany

Jim Morrow attends Officer Candidate School, becomes a Second Lieutenant and is assigned to the 551st AAA Bn. They reach Normandy in late July 1944 and chase (trying to keep up with) Patton across Europe.

Jim Morrow told this story: 'My jeep driver and I were scouting for an artillery setup site and we had to pull over and take cover from enemy artillery fire. Both of us were laying underneath the jeep. I looked over and saw my hand balled up in a fist. I extended my fingers and lay my hand flat to get it lower to the ground. When the fire stopped, we continued our mission.'

He also said he was standing in line to be discharged and the officer told him that no one was going to be separated now and everyone was in 'for the duration.'

Birthday Celebration at a Pill Box

One lighter story: My daddy and my Uncle Eb met at a pill box on Normandy Beach on Daddy's birthday. They celebrated with the most expensive bottle of whisky Daddy had bought from a British soldier.

Above, a picture of the pill box taken by Mac Morrow, the son of Eb Morrow, on a trip to Normandy in approximately 2017.

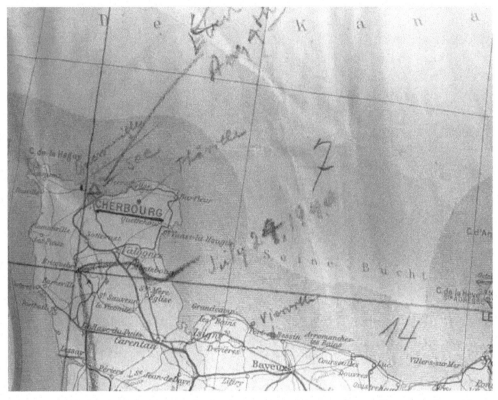

Above, at top left of this map marked with a triangle, the place where brothers Jim and
Eben Morrow met and celebrated Jim's birthday on August 4th, 1944.
The place where Jim Morrow had landed on July 24, 1944 is marked with the date.

Back Home After the War

I found this letter (shown at right) to Daddy in his files. It is from Mrs. Harriet Towers dated February 2, 1958. The postal service delivered mail then without all the "codes" they need now (see envelope below).

Daddy knew "everyone" in the county and had written Mrs. Towers about selling property in Brevard for an Army Reserve Center (the one located on East French Broad Street across from Brevard College). In her letter she indicated someone had discussed the sale of the property before.

The Warranty Deed is dated October 27, 1958, from the Towers to the United States of America and a sales price of $15,000.00.

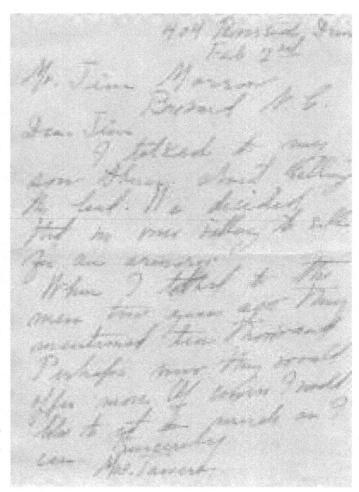

Photograph and article
(at right)
from the Ecusta Paper
Corp. newspaper the
"The Echo" about the
Army Reserves.

Capt. Morrow is pictured
with his hat angled
showing his black hair.
Look just to the left
behind the flag.

Names are listed for
Brevard Army Reserve
Unit.

Leeman Ray Pegram, U.S. Army Air Corps

Staff Sergeant Ray Pegram, Radio Operator, age 20 or 21

Ray Pegram joined the Army in January, 1942 and served in England, France, Holland, and Germany until September, 1945

Ray Pegram's Beginnings

Ray Pegram tells about his life: "I was born in Gerton, North Carolina (near Chimney Rock) in 1923. Then we lived on a farm in Frog Level, N.C..

Ray's first church, Bear Wallow Baptist Church, in Gerton, N.C.

"I was always interested in airplanes. You know the Wright brothers made the first powered flight in 1903 right here in my state, at Kitty Hawk. When I was a teenager, Tom Moore, a friend I grew up with, and I traveled every chance we got to cities where we could see planes. We'd hitchhike to Marion, N.C. because they had a little airport. We'd look at the planes. Or we'd hitchhike to Spartanburg, S.C., or Charlotte, N.C.—anywhere they had airplanes. I was just fascinated with airplanes.

"When I finished high school I got a job as a shipping clerk with Elmore Corporation in Spindale, N.C. We made industrial sewing thread and mercerized thread for women's hose. That was before hose were made from nylon.

"I joined the Army Air Corps in January, 1942, and went to Radio School in Kansas City. They found out I could type, so I never had to pull guard duty or anything.

"I learned to fly in a Link Trainer (a training device on the ground). When we were fooling around in England before D-Day, I sat in the co-pilot's seat and flew a C-47 with a pilot. A C-47 takes off at 90 miles an hour. I took off and made a couple of turns. He asked me if I wanted to land it, and I said, 'No, sir. I'll let you land it. I don't want to get us killed!"I was sent to Columbus, Ohio, Dalhart, Texas, and to Kansas City to the T.W.A. Radio School.

Calisthenics at T.W.A.'s Conditioning School in Kansas City, Missouri April 28, 1943. The soldiers spelled out "T.W.A." with a large "V" for victory at the bottom. Ray said, "I'm in there somewhere." The tall structure in the background is a World War I monument.

42

"We went to Alliance, Nebraska, in February of '43, and was it ever cold! We said there was nothing between us and the North Pole but a barbed wire fence, and it had fallen down," Ray laughed. "When we walked from the barracks up to the hangar, we had to flick the ice out of our noses. That's how cold it was.

"We went to Fort Wayne, Indiana, Presque Isle, Maine and Goose Bay, Newfoundland. Then on to Iceland, Ireland, and we landed in England on October 7, 1943. The English were getting Aldermaston Air Base ready for us. We were the first troop carrier group to land in England. Obviously the planning for D-Day was going on in '43, well ahead of the June '44 invasion. It took a lot of time to get all the troops there and ready."

The D-Day Invasion

"I was in the 434th Troop Carrier Group, 71st Squadron. We dropped the 101st Airborne Division. We carried glider planes, supplies, and paratroops called Pathfinders over Normandy on D-Day, June 6, 1944. We also landed on Omaha Beach and evacuated soldiers.

"We were told on June 4th that we would invade on June 6th. [The D-Day Invasion was originally planned for June 5th, but was delayed one day because of weather].

Vice Air Marshall Mallory [Sir Trafford Leigh-Mallory, British Army, Commander-in-Chief of the Allied Expeditionary Force for the Invasion of Normandy] speaks from the balcony at right. On the evening of June 5, he is giving a pep talk to the troops on the day before the D-Day invasion. A white arrow points to Ray Pegram (white cap). At the same time, Eisenhower was speaking to the 82nd Airborne and 101st Airborne.

We were 'locked up' from June 4th to June 6th so we couldn't tell anybody when the invasion would happen. They even marched us to and from the mess hall to keep an eye on us.

"The Pathfinders we dropped into Normandy had radio equipment for communication with later flights. When the paratroopers got on the ground, they set up beacons for the planes that came in later. The goal was to try to drop the next paratroopers into the same area.

"We also towed two gliders on D-Day and one on the day after D-Day (June 7). We flew some missions directly across the English Channel. We also flew around the Cherbourg, France peninsula and over Jersey and Guernsey Islands [Channel Islands, England] with the Pathfinders. We landed on Omaha Beach when the tide was out."

C-47 42-24022 'BUTCH'
71ST TROOP CARRIER SQUADRON
434th TROOP CARRIER GROUP

**Above, C-47 is staged at Aldermaston, England for the D-Day invasion.
An enlarged photo of the crew is on the next page.**

"For many months after D-Day, we ferried gasoline and other supplies to Patton's Third Army as he advanced across France. We landed in suitable pastures and fields for unloading. There were no runways. We went almost daily when the weather permitted."

Photo: Crew members from left: Beck, Lockard, Litke, O'Neil, Pegram. Not pictured, Major Glenn Mann, Squadron Commander

Holland Invasion, Supplying Bastogne, and Across-the-Rhine Invasion

Professional photograph of C-47s dropping paratroopers in the Holland invasion in daylight. Ray said, "After the D-Day night mission, it was decided to use daylight for all future drops."

45

At left: Para-pack supplies underneath the C-47, ready "to drop to the boys over the Rhine."

March 24, 1945, Reims, France

Above: Dropping supplies to the 191st Division stranded in Bastogne,

Victory in Europe

"When we got word that the Germans had surrendered on May 8, 1945, we were in Nice, France. We were taking the 101st Paratroopers to Nice for Rest & Recreation after the Battle of Bastogne. This is where the Germans made a push back, encircling our troops. They were cut off and we supplied our troops from the air.

"Now you talk about a wild night. Nobody went to bed that night. We were out on the streets celebrating all night. The French people were there. Everyone was shouting and hugging and having something to drink. People were everywhere.

In Germany to bring back our liberated POWs

"After the war was over we ferried our liberated prisoners out of Germany to Reims, France," Ray recalled. "We built tent cities where they would be checked out medically.

"We also had a tent city in Reims where they put Polish women who had been house servants to the Germans. I think there were 3,000 in one camp. We went up to the fence and talked to some of them who spoke English."

Changing the C-47's engine in
Reims, France in 1945

Ray: "Here's my best friend George V. Egan. George was an Irish Catholic from New York and I'm an old Southern Baptist. We didn't have any problems. George's middle initial stood for Victor, but he said it really meant 'Victory'!"

At left: George "Victory" Egan (on the left)
with Ray Pegram

48

ME
My ship showing Missions
A-80 Rheims France
May 1945

Staff Sergeant Ray Pegram stands on the wing of his ship. Next to his left shoulder are symbols tallying the number of drops (paratroops, gliders, evacuations, and supplies) painted on the fuselage.

Photo at right: Ray (bottom center) is pictured with his three brothers, all of whom served in World War II (two in Europe and two in the Pacific). They all came home alive. A fifth brother was above the age limit to serve.

49

When thanked for saving Western civilization, Ray said, "Well, I never had any idea that we wouldn't win. None of us did. I guess they had drilled it into us. I don't ever remember being scared. I was apprehensive, perhaps. I remember standing in the door between the pilot and co-pilot during some of the drops when flak was bursting all around. But I don't ever remember being afraid. Our squadron lost one plane on D-Day and two planes when we dropped across the Rhine. We were the first group into England before D-Day."

Ray arrived back home in July, 1945. After a 30-day furlough, he was sent to Fort Wayne, Indiana, and was scheduled to go to Alliance, Nebraska, to get the C-112, the new airplane that would drop paratroops out of both sides. "We were heading to the Pacific for the invasion of Japan. We were told that there would be a 60% casualty rate. But five of us had our personnel papers misplaced, and we had to stay in Indiana. That turned out to be good because while were still sitting at Fort Wayne, the atomic bombs were dropped in Japan and the war in the Pacific was over. Dropping the bombs saved our lives."

After the War

Ray was discharged from the Army Air Corps on September 2, 1945, at age 23. He returned to Elmore Corporation, the company where he had worked before enlisting. His boss offered him two options—a good job at the company or time to go to college for four years with the promise of a job when he graduated. Ray took the job. For a total of 47 years (including the time before his service in the Army), Ray progressed upward through many jobs to become treasurer, vice president of sales, and for 14 years, company president. He retired at 65 but was offered a sales position by a yarn manufacturing company and worked there in sales until age 78.

Ray remembered, "Someone asked me where I went to college. I said, 'F.L.U.' The person asked, 'Where's that? I never heard of it.' I said, 'Well, that's Frog Level University, grades one through seven. Then I went to high school and worked for Elmore. Then the war came along. I've never been to college.' The person said, 'Didn't hurt you at all, did it?' I said, 'No, sir. It didn't hurt me a bit.'"

Ray and Madge Hardin, who was from Spindale, married in 1946. Sadly, she passed away in 2003. They have a son and a daughter.

Commemorating D-Day

Ray has made four trips to France, England, Holland, Belgium, and Germany since 2012 for commemorations of the events that defeated the Germans in 1945. He has made many friends on those trips and stays in touch with them. One French friend, Valerie Gautier Cardin, texts with him every day.

In 2015 Ray took his daughter, son, and their spouses to Holland, and to Aldermaston, England, and Omaha Beach, France. In Aldermaston, they were able to see the place on the hill where Eisenhower planned the D-Day invasion.

Ray sits in a C-47 in 2016 during a commemoration of D-Day near Omaha Beach.

During the commemoration, paratroopers dropped in honor of the paratroopers of 1944.

Ray said, "They kept coming for hours."

At right is a limited-edition print of a painting by Larry Selman. It honors the troops who dropped into Sainte-Mere-Eglise in Normandy on D-Day.

Ray was asked to sign the 200 prints as a member of one of the C-47 crews being depicted in the painting. At left, he signs a print in his kitchen in Spindale, N.C.

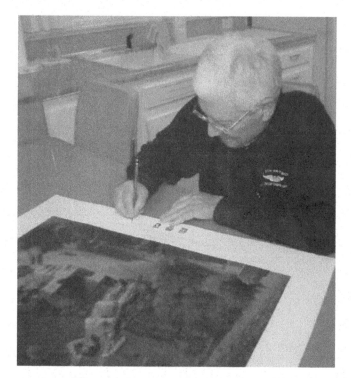

52

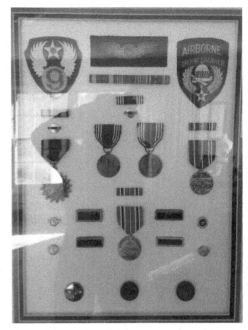

At right, Ray's insignia and medals. He was awarded the Air Medal with two oak leaf clusters, the Good Conduct Medal, the European Victory Medal, the American Victory Medal, and the French Legion of Honor Medal.

Included are Unit Lead Crew badges and Unit Citation for Performance.

At a ceremony on Utah Beach on the Normandy coast, Ray was awarded the French Legion of Honor Medal. Ray is shown at left holding the medal in 2016.

Ray said, "It seems to me that if you were involved in D-Day, you're still alive, and the French can find you, they're going to give you that award."

Dorothy Schieve, U.S. Army, Womens' Army Corps

Sergeant Dorothy Wilson Schieve, Women's Army Corps

Dorothy Wilson Schieve joined the Army at age 18—April,1942. She served in England and was working in Paris during its liberation. She was discharged in May, 1945.

Dorothy tells her story: "I was born in Van, Texas, but my family moved east for an oil drilling boom when I was five. My dad was in charge of building the railroad. When I was 18, we were living in Texarkana, and I joined the Army. You were supposed to be 21. My brother was in the Air Force. He wasn't going to get anything on me. I joined and said I was 21. And I got away with it. It was sort of iffy there for a while with my mother, but finally my brother, who was a flier, talked to Mother. He said, 'She can convince them that she's 28 instead of 18.' And that was it. She refused keep me home any more.

"Jack and I grew up together and we were a twosome. I had another brother, James, 18 years older and a sister, Mary, 12 years older, but Jack was only four years older. We stuck together. I wouldn't do something if Jack didn't approve of it. If I had a date with a boy he didn't approve, he'd say, 'No, you're not going to go with him,' and I wouldn't. I listened to him."

Dorothy and her siblings: from left, Dorothy, Jack, Mary, and James.
This photo was taken on the day Dorothy left for the Army.
Jack took Dorothy to the train. He was Dorothy's real pal.

In the Army

"I went to basic training in Louisiana. The place had been built for a Japanese camp, but it had never been used for that. I had been there four weeks, when on the P.A. system, they said, 'Private Dorothy Wilson, report to the Commandant immediately.' I thought, 'They found out.' I was scared to death. I went in and this lady said, 'What I'm going to tell you, you can't tell anybody. You can't repeat it. We're offering you Officers Candidate School. You have 24 hours to think about it. You're excused.' I had been in only four weeks.

"I left and went back to my class. The other girls asked me, 'What did you do?' I said, 'I forgot to sign a paper.' Later on that day, another announcement: 'Dorothy Wilson, please report to the Commandant's office.' I thought, 'They've caught me. They know how old I am.' Another lady in uniform was there said, 'What I'm going to tell you, you cannot repeat it. You have been chosen to go overseas. You have 24 hours to think about it.' So that's what I did. That's what I chose."

Overseas Duty in Europe

"And away I went the next day. They came in a truck. I was the only one going. I went to an Army base in southern Louisiana. There were men there, too. The women were enclosed in barbed wire and we could not go out singly. We had to have somebody walk with us. From there we got on a train that took us to St. Louis. We thought, 'This is it.' They got us off the train, marched us around, and then put us back on the train. So we knew 'OK, this wasn't it.' And away we went to Massachusetts. We were there quite a while preparing to go overseas.

"Someone in the legislature said, 'We can't send women overseas.' At that time we were the WAAC—Women's Army Auxiliary Corps. They changed it to WACS—Women's Army Corps. Finally, we went to New York and got on ships. Two of the platoons got on these great big ships. Our platoon was last, and we got on an old boat that had been a cruise ship. We had to sleep in hammocks hanging from the ceiling. My last name was Wilson, so I was the last one to be assigned. I slept third up, right next to the ceiling of this old pleasure boat that was no pleasure. You had to climb up on the two lower swinging hammocks.

"This room was also where we ate. Twice a day, we would take our eating containers and go down the line, taking whatever foods we wanted. We ate as we kept walking and were finished eating by the time we got to the end. At the end were two barrels—one with soapy water where we washed our dishes and one with clear water to rinse them. We didn't sit down to eat. That was our meal. Right there under those hammocks.

"We were in a convoy. It was foggy and you couldn't see anything for days. There was a destroyer going around and around us trying to get us to go faster. We were the slowest.

It took us forever and a day. When we finally arrived in England, they had built these high steps to get us off this boat, because it had no opening at the bottom. When we came into port, we rammed the heck out of that platform and it fell apart. So we didn't have any way to get off the boat. If you've ever seen 20 girls cry—we were dirty, hungry. The ship turned around and went to another docking place and they finally got us off the ship. We were thrilled. Some commandant wanted us to go to breakfast and tell us how great it was for us to be there. All we wanted to do was sleep. It was 4:30 in the morning!

"Then we were sent to London. That's where we found out that the first and second platoons had had to turn around and go back to Canada because the ship was smoking. It was two months before they got to England. We got plum jobs by being there first. I was assigned to the European Theatre Operation-U.S. Army. They decided to make the Supreme Headquarters there and had called back some retired generals. I became secretary to Colonel Smith. Eisenhower came from Africa and formed the Supreme Headquarters Allied Expeditionary Force, which was called SHAEF."

Typing Code

"I was assigned there to Staff Message Control at Bushy Park. They had put tin Quonset huts there. There were four typists sitting at a table. It was all coded. My shift was 11 pm to 7 am. It was cold and damp. We lived there in Bushy Park in separate quarters. We had to type constantly because we had to fill in the whole time. If we didn't have anything to type, we typed nursery rhymes, anything we could think of. We had to do that because the Germans could de-code it. So we had to keep somebody typing for literally 24 hours. Each day there were three shifts. We had a hard time sleeping during the day because the other girls were coming back to the bunks when they got off.

"When I had a few days off, I took a trip to Scotland just for fun. When I got back I was re-assigned to London. In London I lived in an apartment and ate in restaurants. I was warm. I was in a typing pool. I was sent to Major Mayborn, who was head of public relations. He was known to have a little temper. He had had four secretaries come and go. When I was assigned there, they said, 'Oh, another one!' So I was assigned to him IF he wanted to keep me. I went down to his office. He asked me where I was from. I said, 'Texas.' He said, 'I'm from Texas!' And we hit it off great. He even gave me away when I got married.

"We five WACS stayed in an apartment building in London. We were getting the buzz bombs. We'd hear them go put-put-put. When you heard them click, you had 15 seconds to take cover. One morning about seven o'clock, I was at the lavatory in front of a window. I heard the put-put-put. My roommate, Jean, said, 'Is that a motorcycle or a bomb?' I had just seen a motorcycle go down the street and thought that's what it was. But then we heard the click.

"The building had three floors. We were on the second. We tried to get under the beds. Jeannie was a bit plump. We got her head under the bed. There was an explosion. We were in the center, which was the safest place. All around us, fifty American soldiers were killed and 100 were injured badly. We could hear them screaming, 'Help me, help me. I've lost my arm. Come get me!' Jeannie and I helped them. When the bomb blew up there was dirt all over the place. They moved us out to Bushy Park until they found another place for us.

"At Bushy Park, I met my future husband. A friend of mine was dating his roommate. One night, my friend said, 'Come on, let's go. They're playing baseball.' She said her friend would bring his roommate, George. I said no. She said, 'Oh, come on. You don't have anything else to do.' So I went. That's how I met him. We dated a couple of times and then my group was transferred back to London. George had to take his company down to the south of England where the ships were going out to France. So I kind of forgot about him and we didn't see each other for a long time."

Transfer to Paris

"The other WACS and I got the word 'Pack your bags. Do not tell your lieutenant. Just pack and be ready to go. We had these musette bags and the big bags going bump-bump-bump down the stairs. The lieutenant heard all this and came out and asked, 'Where are you going?' We said, 'We don't know.' She said, 'You can't go!' We said, 'Yes, ma'am, we can.' And we got in the back of this truck and took off for the airport and flew to Paris. We flew very low, so if they shot us, we didn't have very far to fall," Dorothy joked.

"When we got to Paris, it was the day before Paris was liberated. We worked on the fourth floor of the American Express building, which was right across the street from the opera house. We heard a gunshot, so we went out to look. There was a ledge on the outside of the windows. We saw a French man with a gun chasing a German down the middle of the street. He had found him in the basement of the opera house. The Resistance were looking for Germans and shooting them. On the ledge, we were saying, 'Come on!' and cheering the Frenchman on. Major Mayborn came out and said, 'What are you doing out here? You could be shot!'

"One night we were eating dinner at our hotel, the Scribe Hotel. There were five of us girls around the table. My friend, Jean, saw a man standing in the doorway. She said, 'Dorothy, that man in the doorway is staring at you.' I turned around and saw six-foot, one-inch George. He was stationed at Versailles at the time and had come to Paris.

"Versailles was where the main Supreme Headquarters was. George came over and talked to me. We made a date for the next night and we started going out again. He had a Jeep and a driver. So we went around, all over. He was a company commander, an officer; I was enlisted. We weren't supposed to fraternize. But we enjoyed fraternizing very much. George was a commanding officer. He was head of the grocery store for generals.

1st Lt. George Schieve

"One day, I was called to General Allen's office. I couldn't imagine what I had done! When I got there, General Allen had a cake. He asked me if I knew the name Lt. Schieve. I said yes. He said, 'I was at his store to get some groceries today. Lt. Schieve and I started talking, and he told me about you. He gave me this cake. I want you to take it for you and the other girls.' Later, I was called to his office again (on the loud speaker), and he had a box of cupcakes. We enjoyed eating those cupcakes! After that, every time General Allen saw me, he would tease me, 'Have you seen the grocery man?' General Allen came to my wedding."

Public Relations

"In the public relations office, we would get letters from Washington when the reporters wanted to come over from the U.S. to write stories about the war. It was Major Mayborn's job to decide who could come and where they would be assigned and for how long. It was my job to type the orders, so every one of them had to come to my desk. I met Dorothy Kilgallen, Edward R. Murrow, and so many others. It was really interesting—this girl from Texas. By this time, I think I was nineteen! But they all had to come to me.

"One time I walked by General Allen's office where he and Edward R. Murrow were talking. General Allen called out to me, 'Hey you. Would you take a letter?' His secretary was away. I took the letter and ran upstairs to my office to type it on my own typewriter. When I finished, I took it in to my boss, Major Mayborn and asked him to check it. He said, 'I don't see any errors, but who is this letter to?' I had left that off. So I ran back up to General Allen's office to ask who the letter was to. I was embarrassed by my mistake in leaving that out of the letter. General Allen said, 'Little lady, it's all settled. We don't need the letter after all.' I turned around and ran right smack into Major Mayborn. He had come to 'save' me from any negative consequences of my error, but there weren't any. Everything was OK.

"Some of the reporters were so nasty. There was one I would have loved to have thrown out. His wife was there. She was working for some magazine. She said something to me that was very complimentary, and her husband said sarcastically, 'Oh, that's her job.' I thought, 'This guy—I'll get back at him if it's the last thing I do.' After they left, I went to Major Mayborn and asked, 'What are you going to do with him?' He said, 'Oh, I'll send him out for six weeks or so.' I told him what had happened, so Major Mayborn cut it short, so instead of six weeks, they could only stay maybe two weeks. Fortunately, I don't know his name. But I got my revenge. His wife was so nice, though. She was interested in women, particularly in Germany. Whether she got to go to Germany, I don't know."

My Brother Jack, the Pilot

"My brother Jack was a B-17 pilot. I saw him a few times over there. His plane was shot down on the border of Germany and Holland. The crew members were taken prisoner by the Germans, but all the officers, including Jack, who was the pilot, were hanged. He, the navigator, and the bombardier. They had wanted my brother to teach because he'd been flying since he was 15 years old. But he wanted to fly.

"Jack had graduated from high school when he was 15 and went to University of Texas for one year. He came home at the end of the year and said, 'OK, that's it. I'm not going to go back.' Dad said, 'What do you want to do?' Jack said, 'I want to learn to fly.' Every Saturday, Jack had taken our truck from this little town that we lived in, to Tyler, Texas, to get fresh veggies and bring them back for the grocery store that Dad owned. While he was in Tyler, he would go out to the airfield. The owners would take him up. They taught him to fly, but he couldn't fly solo because he was too young. That was how he started flying."

A Wedding in Paris

"Just before Christmas in Paris, we tried to buy gifts to send back to the States, but none of us spoke French, and the clerks in the stores didn't speak English, so that was challenging.

"George and I got married in the American Cathedral in Paris, one week before the war ended. General Mayborn walked me down the aisle. We stayed in Paris until the war ended. We knew we would be separated when the war ended. George said, 'I'm not going to let you go!'"

George wanted Dorothy to buy some civilian clothes (photo above) when they were married in 1945. He had only seen her in her uniform.

The War in Europe Ends

"I was discharged from the Army after V-E Day and came back home to Texas. George stayed in Europe until the end of August and helped get all these soldiers back home. He stayed in the Army for another year. We were still fighting in the Pacific and he was needed. He was quartermaster. When he came back to the States, we lived in an apartment near the airfield in New Jersey. He was discharged in Chicago. My WACS roommate, Jean, lived in Chicago, so I was able to stay with her for a couple of days when George and I went out there."

Civilian Life

"George had already graduated from college when he went into the service. He was a bit older than I. Six years I think. He didn't really know how old I was. When he found out, he probably thought, 'I'm marrying a teeny-bopper!' Anyway, he had graduated from Michigan State University and he found a job immediately when he got out of the Army as a hospital administrator—at a mental hospital outside Ann Arbor.

"We had housing provided there on the hospital grounds (the home is pictured above).George was hired as the assistant manager, but the manager became ill, and George was asked to become the manager of this 500-bed hospital. It was a good situation. We had maid service and lots of other children of the doctors and psychiatrists for our children to play with. We had a swimming pool and two tennis courts. The kids went to school at Eastern Michigan University Lab School. I couldn't believe that I had married into all that!"

Below: Dorothy and George and their children (from left) Jane, Mary, and Ron

"We had three children: Ron, Jane, and Mary. After the kids were in college, I was bored and decided that I would go back to work. I worked at the University of Michigan Medical School in Ann Arbor. I was an administrative assistant with a staff of two.

"George stayed in that job in Michigan until his retirement. He had always wanted to live in Arizona. So we moved to Arizona, but found it too hot and George was bored. So he got another job in Indianapolis and went back to work as a hospital superintendent for the state of Indiana. We were there for 10 years. Then we retired to Florida. Sadly, George passed away 20 years ago. I still miss him. He was a great guy."

"My son and his wife live in Brevard. He asked me to move to Brevard, so I moved here four years ago. I miss seeing my daughters. One lives in Michigan and one lives in Arizona, but they come to visit. I like it here."

Dorothy Schieve in 2019

George Sarros, U.S. Navy

Motor Machinist 3rd Class George Sarros, U.S. Navy

George Sarros was drafted into the U.S. Navy in June, 1943. He served in the engine room on an LST before and during the D-Day invasion, and through the war's end. He was discharged in March, 1946.

George Sarros was born in Chicago in 1925. He was an 18-year-old high school senior when his draft papers came, but President Roosevelt had just issued a statement saying that students with six months left to finish high school, you could be deferred. Nevertheless George went to the recruiting office in Chicago, passed the physical, and showed the "deferral" article to the officer. He told the officer he wanted to be in the Navy, not the Army, and it worked. He went into the Navy.

Preparing for the Invasion: April, 1944

Over the second half of 1943 and the first half of 1944 . . . thousands of new American soldiers, sailors, and airmen were pouring into Britain every week, to make a total of some 1.6 million British-based American troops by the eve of the Normandy invasion.

In early November, 1943, the 3,000 residents of Slapton (near center of map, left), a small village in the rich farmland on England's east coast, were told they would have to evacuate by Christmas.

They moved their families, livestock, pets, and farm equipment to make way for the Americans. Slapton was part of a twenty-five square mile area known as South Hams, which had been requisitioned under the 1939 War Powers Act for training of the American troops who would invade Normandy. This area was chosen for training because its terrain was very similar to the area on the Normandy coast which became known as Omaha Beach (from *Exercise Tiger,* by Nigel Lewis).

George Sarros was a motor machinist on an LST* (Landing Ship, Tanks) which would be landing tanks, vehicles, cargo, and troops directly onto shore with no docks or piers. Some LSTs had as many as 18 guns.

George worked in the engine room of LST number 515, which was one of seven ships in the group called Exercise Tiger. They trained on the English coast and prepared for the invasion of Normandy. 515 was the lead ship in the flotilla.

LST 515, Photo credit: Exercise Tiger by Nigel Lewis, Prentice Hall Press

*The sailors also called these ships "Ts" or "Last Stranded Target" or "Last Slow Target."

Above, LST 515's Engineering Group
Dark-haired George Sarros is pictured in second row seated, second from left.

In detail of group photo below, George is pictured on top row, center.

On April 28, 1944, less than six weeks before D-Day, the ships of Exercise Tiger were attacked by German E-Boats. (E stood for enemy.) George remembers, "Our boat was the lead boat. We had the commander aboard our ship. We were on maneuvers in the English Channel. We were supposed to land on Slapton Sands. There was supposed to be an English destroyer with us, but for some reason, the communication failed and the destroyer wasn't there.

"Just after midnight, we were called up to General Quarters. Our sister ship 507 had been torpedoed. Then another ship was torpedoed. Then another one. The commander told us to head for the beach. But my captain, Captain John Doyle (pictured at right), said 'No, we're going to pick up survivors.' He was a hero for making that decision.

"So while we were trying to pick up survivors, the Germans were coming after us. They sent a couple of torpedoes to our ship but missed us. "We opened gunfire and shot as much as we could, but it was pitch dark. You couldn't see your hand in front of you.

LST 515 Captain John Doyle Photo credit: *Exercise Tiger* by Nigel Lewis

"So we lowered our small LCVP [landing craft, vehicle personnel] boats to rescue the survivors. We had a young man by the name of McCann on there. McCann was only 15 years old. He had a lantern he'd taken from an officer's cabin, so he could see the survivors. He had been a fisherman from California. I think we picked up about 100 survivors.

Joseph McCann, age 15 Photo credit: *Exercise Tiger* by Nigel Lewis

"In order to bring them inside, we had nets. But they were wounded, so they couldn't climb up the nets. So we opened up the doors where the small boats could bring them up. We would take them into the ship, and then the small boats would go out and pick up more survivors.

70

"A lot of the people we picked up were dead. We lost maybe 1000 people from those ships that were torpedoed. The oil and the fumes exploded. We took one guy that we rescued and put him on the table where we ate. We tried to revive him, but he never made it. So we had to take his dog tags and his wallet. We opened it up and saw a picture of his wife.

"I don't know how many we had that died, but we were lucky. We were a lucky ship. And my captain, he was from Texas. If it wasn't for him deciding to stay and rescue [rather than follow orders to return to port], a lot of these guys wouldn't have survived."

George then read aloud from the book *Exercise Tiger*, quoting a sailor who was in the ship 506. "It was a high, roaring furnace fire. Cans of gasoline on crowded, canvas-covered trucks are exploding. Balls of fire and small-arms ammunition are exploding, but the greatest horror is the agonizing screams for help of the trapped men. They were in the tank deck."

George continued, "It all exploded, and none of those guys had a chance to get out. See, I didn't know this was going on. I didn't know how bad it was because we were the lead ship. A lot of the men in the water had life belts on around here (George pointed to his waist.), so when the explosion happened, and it blew them out in the water, they were unconscious. They were just lying in the water face down. If they'd had a Mae West suit with a collar, they would have floated [with their faces out of the water] even if they were knocked out. But the water was 45 degrees.

"We picked up one guy who was floating all by himself. We thought he was dead. The only thing that had kept him alive was that he was so fat, so he was floating higher. It was dark, so we couldn't tell. But he wasn't dead."

LST 289 (above)was badly damaged, but was taken into port, repaired, and put back into commission. Photo credit: Walter Trombold and *Exercise Tiger*, by Nigel Lewis

"One guy on a burning ship didn't have a life belt. He was a corporal, I think. He was scared and kept saying, 'Don't leave me. Don't leave me. I don't want to die.' He was holding onto another guy. The other guy said, 'Just hold onto me. We'll jump together.' So they jumped. The guy without the life belt saw some piece of wood and started hanging onto that. The other guy said, 'No, don't stay there [near the ship]. When that ship goes down it will suck you down with it. So he tried to get the corporal off the wood. The corporal wouldn't let go, so the other guy had to swim away. He said he felt so bad.

"Then they told us German E-boats were coming after us, 'Hold your fire. Hold your fire." Then the tower was telling us how close the boats were coming in to try to torpedo us. Then when the boats got into a certain point, the tower said, 'Open fire.' We had 40 MMs and we just shot up as much as we could. I was a loader. I was loading clips into the guns. One of the fellas said he saw a torpedo go by our bow. We never got hit. We survived. But, I'll tell you, we were shaken.

"I remember guys in the water yelling, 'Help me, help me.' We would yell back, 'Hang on. We're gonna pick you up. The small boat's coming. Just hang on. Hang on, mate. Hang on, mate.'

"I think a lot of them who died was because of exposure in the 45-degree water. We were out there till about 5:00 or 6:00 in the morning. When we took these guys into port, we were told that we couldn't talk about what had happened. We couldn't say anything.

"We weren't allowed to talk about it until 1958 when this book (*Exercise Tiger*) was published. I suppose they didn't want the Germans to know what was going on."

D-Day

"We were supposed to invade France on June 5, but the weather was too bad. We sailed just after midnight on the morning of June 6. Our ship was full of engineers, tanks, and trucks. We didn't hit the beach until 1:00 pm June 6. When we hit the beach, we had a German fighter come down and try to strafe us. But no sooner did he come down but a P-47 was right on his tail. And just blew him right out of the water.

"Our biggest problem was the German mines that were in the water. When you're sailing, the props in the water brings those mines up and just blows the tail of the ship apart. Where we used to eat lunch was in the tail, and we used to sleep back there, so the skipper told us, "You're now moving your stuff on the side of the ship'. So now our bunks were on the side of the ship.

"Sometimes when we sailed from England to France, we had to have an escort to locate submarines. They sent depth charges down. We didn't know it, we started running for the ladder, and then they told us it was just a depth charge. We thought we'd been hit.

"We had a blimp attached to our ship and floating above it – a big balloon. When the Germans planes tried to attack us, they'd hit the blimp. It protected us. When we landed on the beach, the German plane was coming down on us, but our bomber was right on his tail and got him.

"On D-Day, we landed and unloaded, and then we took the wounded back. On the tank deck, we could put 400-500 stretchers there. The ambulance trucks would come with the wounded, and our guys would get out and help the wounded onto our ship. "We'd take our wounded back to England and get them into hospitals. We took German prisoners too. We kept them in the tank deck; they couldn't go anywhere else.

"Our planes had gone into Normandy much earlier – about 1:00 in the morning, dropping the paratroopers.

Ambulance being loaded onto an LST in England, to be taken to France to rescue the wounded Allies

Their job was to knock out German communications and bridges. When we landed, we took a bunch of those paratroopers back to England. Some of them had picked up German lugers and swords and brought them with them.

"We took quite a few German prisoners. The young German soldiers were determined that they were going to win. The older ones were just glad the war was almost over."

Battle of the Bulge and End of the War

George continued, "I remember when we took brand-new soldiers going to the Battle of the Bulge. Their numbers were still on their helmets. They were as young as I was — eighteen years old. We were losing the battle over there. That was around Christmas time. The weather was bad. You couldn't fly because you couldn't see.

"I was still in England when the war ended — Southampton. We were on the ship. We knew the war would be ending soon. We used to get on the train when we got liberty and go into town. I didn't have enough points to get out of service. When I finally came back, my brother was in the hospital in Norfolk, so I got to visit him."

After the War

"I met my wife, Enrica, in Chicago. She was a nurse and I was a bartender. She wanted to move to Hawaii. That was her idea. She was a nurse, and she went to Hawaii first and got a job in a hospital. A year later, I followed her there and got a job as a bartender in a country club with a wonderful floor show. We got married. I was 35 years old. We came back to the mainland in 1964, lived in California, then Oregon. I worked as a postal carrier. We went on a mission for our church to Washington, D.C., and then back to Oregon. We adopted two sons, David and Terry. They both live in Colorado now and have families.

"Enrica and I moved to Flat Rock, N.C. in 2001. Sadly, she passed away in 2007. I belong to a church, and that keeps me going.

"Some buddies and I went back to Normandy. The cemeteries. You just cry. You see grave markers that no one knows. The marker just says, 'God knows.' It makes you cry."

**George Sarros at home in
Flat Rock, N.C. in 2018**

1st Lt. Seymour Smolen, U.S. Army

1st Lt. Seymour Smolen, Tank Commander, U.S. Army, D-Day

1st Lt. Sy Smolen served from 1942-1945 in the U.S. Army.
He took his tank onto Utah Beach on D-Day and became de facto Commander
when he was the only officer left in the company.

Story written by Carl Burkhart, Sy Smolen's son-in-law:

There is a group photo on my wall, from my wife's side of the family. It was taken a couple of years before Sy Smolen died. In the photo are 31 people, including Sy, who sits in the middle leaning on his cane. But for three factors—the right landing beach, an Army medic, and a bump from an airplane at the last minute—19 of the 31 people in the photo would not exist.

From the Garment District to Officer Candidate School to D-Day

Sy was in the rag trade, working with his dad and brother in the garment district of New York City. At the beginning of the war he got himself drafted. He went to OCS, became an officer, and learned all about Sherman tanks.

His young wife left their baby daughter (later my wife) with her mother in the city, and followed Sy across the country. Sy's destiny was sealed, however, when he was transferred to England. His tank battalion evacuated, then occupied, the small town of Torcross on the southwest coast. They practiced landings on the adjacent long, narrow beach of Slapton Sands.

On D-Day, June 6th, 1944, Sy took his tank ashore in the first wave on Utah Beach.

Luck of the Draw #1

Sy's group was put ashore at Utah Beach. A larger percentage of Shermans at Omaha Beach were offloaded too far from the shore, or were otherwise incapacitated or destroyed in the first wave.

When they cleared the beach, Sy found himself the only officer left in the company and became de facto company commander. They survived that day…then the next…then the next, as they headed inland through the hedgerows of Normandy.

Then, as Sy described it in a letter home, 'One sunny afternoon while flanking the city of Montebourg in advance of our infantry, things started to get hot. We fought to the outskirts and then unfortunately I got hit. It felt just like having someone throw hot water on me. I turned over my command, bailed out of my tank, and sent them on.' He was horribly wounded in the left side of his head and left for dead.

Luck of the Draw #2

A medic saw signs of life and treated him. He was evacuated to a hospital in England for further treatment. Sy had lost his left eye. His head was mangled and full of shrapnel. By mid-July, recovering in an English hospital, he was expecting to be sent home in a few days. But he was bumped from his flight at the last minute to make room for a VIP.

Luck of the Draw #3

That flight went down over the Atlantic, cause unknown. Sy finally made it back to the States and to an Indiana hospital for rehabilitation and plastic surgery. By mid-1945, he was with his family and working again in the rag trade. He had a glass eye and a well-reconstructed face. He fathered two sons and another daughter…and they, along with my wife, are the source of most of the people in the family photo.

After Sy's death, cleaning out his Florida condo, we came upon a set of glass eyes the Army has issued him: a yellow one for jaundice and a bloodshot one for hangovers, among others. They wanted him to be able to match the good right eye no matter what the occasion. But Sy always wore the crystal-clear eyeball in the left socket.

One Christmas about twenty years ago, I joined his sons and another son-in-law for a night at the pool hall. Sy came along for the ride. His oldest son challenged him to a game. Sy cleaned his clock! Guess what form of rehabilitation they had given the one-eyed guys at the Indiana hospital."

Seymour Smolen, 57 years after D-Day and still kicking

Verl Edward Luzena, U. S. Army Air Force

PFC Verl Luzena in Photographic Training

Verl Luzena joined the Army on July 22, 1942 and served in the Army Air Force 4th Combat Camera Unit, Ninth Air Force. He was discharged November 15, 1945.

December 7, 1941: Pearl Harbor

Verl Luzena was a junior at Miami University of Ohio when the Japanese attacked Pearl Harbor. He was spending time with friends in his dormitory, when someone came in with news he had heard on the radio: America had been attacked. Some of those friends talked and agreed that day that they would join the service. "We thought we would be drafted. A number of us decided to volunteer," Verl said.

Verl joined the U.S. Army on July 22, 1942 and married Ruth Louise Gray a month later, on August 25. Verl, from Bradford, Ohio, and Ruth, from Oil City, Pennsylvania, were both students at Miami University.

In the Army, Verl chose photography when pilot training didn't work out. A family friend had taught him how to use a camera around the time he was twelve, and he'd enjoyed taking pictures ever since. On the family farm, he had snapped photos of chickens, cows, and people—kids in the family. Eventually, he began to photograph wedding services for family members, not taking money, but giving the pictures to the newlyweds.

Verl, center, with his parents back on their farm in Ohio

In Army aptitude tests, he scored 100% in photography every time, so that career path was a natural. This led to his assignment in the 4th Camera Combat Unit, one of only 14 CCUs worldwide during World War II. Camera Combat Units typically had 23-30 cameramen and six officers each.

Photography and Hollywood, Here I Come

After photographic training at Lowry Field in Denver, Verl went on to Hollywood for more training, learning to use a motion picture camera. The Hollywood establishment was making major efforts to support the war effort. Verl and his bride, Ruth, rented an apartment there, and she worked at the Los Angeles Stock Market. Verl took a streetcar to work in Culver City.

Above, Army Air Force Photographic Training Center in Culver City, California

Below, Photographic training in Culver City. Verl is second from right.

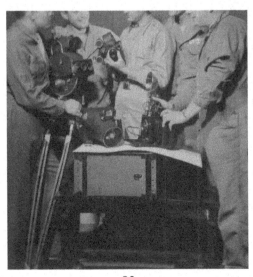

Verl Luzena, while attending his first photography
training at Lowry Field in Denver, Colorado
for 12 weeks.

In Hollywood, Verl and Ruth often had opportunities to socialize and rub elbows with movie folks. Verl remembers standing in line next to Alan Ladd and seeing Mickey Rooney regularly in the cafeteria. Ronald Reagan was paymaster/personnel officer for Verl's unit, and Verl was once asked to give Reagan information about a car accident he had witnessed involving a small boy. He remembers that Reagan, though he didn't know the boy, was very concerned and showed a lot of compassion for the child.

Ronald Reagan, Paymaster for Verl Luzena's Combat Camera Unit

In photographic training, Verl made the point with his superiors that none of the cameramen knew how to repair their equipment, and "They should know their cameras the way an infantryman knows his rifle". As a result, Verl was sent around to various camera manufacturers to learn how to repair the equipment. He then trained other cameramen.

He requested to be sent to Europe rather than remaining stateside, and embarked for Scotland in April, 1944. But in New York City, he had an unexpected delay. So he contacted Ruth, who jumped on a train and went to New York. They stayed at the Taft Hotel, each morning not knowing if he would be called to board the ship or would delay another day.

This went on for a while until they both decided they couldn't take one more day, so they said goodbye. Verl did, in fact, go into quarantine for departure that very day, so their decision was a wise one. He was initially based in England at an airfield filming the daily departure and return of bombing missions.

D-Day: My Plan Was to Shoot Him Before He Could Shoot Me

Verl was a cameraman coming in on a ship on D-Day, at 11:00 the night of June 6, 1944, attached to an engineering unit. The 4th Combat Camera Unit was dispersed; some came in with the paratroopers, some with the gliders, and so forth. Approaching the beach, the ship next to his struck a mine which blew off the front half of the boat, killing most of those aboard. Later, further in, he remembers being told by an officer not to move, else he would get shot, by friendly fire if not the enemy, as two sentries nearby had just shot each other. He carried two weapons: a .45 [pistol] and a rifle. "But I never shot either one of them," Verl remembered. More importantly, he carried two motion picture cameras—one black & white and one color—and a still camera.

He recalls taking cover under a generator truck the first night. After a German fighter made a belly landing in the field next to him, he stayed awake all night watching in case the pilot had survived and might take aim at him. He said, "My plan was to shoot him before he could shoot me."

On the third day after the landing, Verl spotted a large plume of smoke and decided to investigate. After walking half a mile, he met two soldiers, one badly wounded and being helped by his buddy, desperately looking for a medic. The wounded soldier had a two-foot shard of metal clean through him, protruding from his stomach, and still hot enough to be steaming. Verl told them there were no medics where he had come from and they should look in a different direction.

Shortly, Verl came to a forest of metal, heavy metal that had been ripped into long sharp-edged spear-like strips, many taller than him, embedded in the macadam road, and standing straight up, clearly having rained down from above. He had to zig and zag to get through.

Verl soon came to the inferno causing all of this. One of the major allied ammo dumps had somehow caught fire and munitions were periodically exploding. Verl took shelter in a ditch and found he was sharing it with an all-black unit. Another group was fighting the fire, trying to save the all-important ammunition. They had a large pipe with eight hoses attached, manned by soldiers spraying water on the fire. As Verl filmed, another explosion knocked them all down, killing several. It wasn't long before another group took their place, only to suffer the same fate, and be replaced in turn.

Eventually that night, Verl rejoined his unit, which was based in a barn. Sitting on his cot about 3:00 AM by the light of his flashlight, he wrote a caption to go with the film. At daylight he went down to the beach and found a pilot going back to England who could deliver it.

By a strange coincidence not long after VE day, Verl went back to England with a close buddy in his unit. The buddy was actually a German Jew who had been sent to America for safe harbor, but ended up returning as an American soldier. His father was a bigwig with Pathe News who had managed to remain in Germany, somehow tolerated by the Reich who believed he could help with their image. Anyway, Verl and his buddy went to the cinema, and there in the Pathe newsreel was Verl's footage from the ammunition dump. What he will never forget is hearing the caption read, exactly word-for-word as he had written it that night in the barn.

One time while covering a heavy artillery unit, the commander offered Verl a bunk at the headquarters, but he preferred to base himself near the guns. It was a good choice, since the HQ was badly hit that night, and he might have perished. Asked if he was scared, Verl said, "I was cautious."

A Movie Camers on a Fighter Plane

While he was in France, Verl was involved in inventing ways to mount cameras onto airplanes, including on the wings of fighter planes. He had a friend from home in his unit with whom he had played basketball, who would make the sheet metal brackets and housing he needed to mount the cameras. Sheet metal had been the family business back home. The 35mm motion picture cameras were wired to the guns and aimed with the guns so they captured the results of the shots.

Below: Motion picture camera mounted on wing of bomber, with housing methods developed, improved, and installed (see documentation below) by Verl Luzena

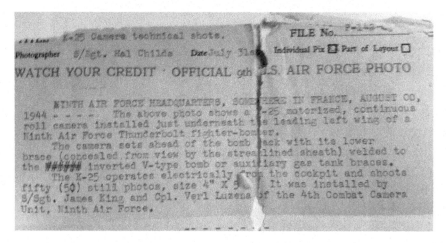

At the end of a bombing run, Verl would pull the film out of the camera and send it to London for developing and showing, in whatever way was needed. "I never got to see it," he said, "but it fed the daily newsreels." A lot of the stock footage we still see today on strafing runs was shot this way. Much later, back at home after the war when his kids were small and watching TV with their dad, he would often recognize bits of his own filming, or his unit's filming, and point it out.

How the Combat Camera Unit Worked

The Combat Camera Unit was a general resource for a large theater of war. It wasn't a cohesive unit that moved around together shooting pictures and film. Instead, individual cameramen or small groups were dispatched to wherever the action was: "You cover this battle, you cover this other one, etc." This led to Verl being present at lots of different campaigns and battles, and as a result, he received lots of medals (unfortunately, now all gone missing). Verl moved about with a fair amount of independence and often had a Jeep. He might be sleeping under a truck during a bombardment one night, or drinking wine at some inn on another.

Army Air Force cameramen and trainees. Verl is front row, third from right.

In Trouble with Ike

Because of this improvised organization, Verl occasionally received notices from Eisenhower's general staff, advising him of events. One time he and another cameraman went to the middle of an empty field where Eisenhower and three other generals were flying in separately for a meeting. They filmed the brief meeting.

When the meeting ended, Eisenhower walked around behind his plane with Verl's partner following him, camera running. Ike reemerged, passing Verl with the comment: "You G.D. Air Force cameramen—I can't even take a pee!"

Verl said, "I saluted him, he saluted me, and went on his way. I kept my mouth shut."

Gen. Eisenhower (stock photo)

Paris, Belgium, and Berlin

Verl was staying with a family in a small town near Paris when the Allies liberated the city. He had gotten to be friends with his host family and had use of a bicycle, so he was able to get to Paris for the historic event. He remembers crowds of people just milling around everywhere, with spontaneous parades breaking out.

He went to the Battle of the Bulge and remembers his group trying to drive through an ice storm. They had to lie on the hood and scrape the windshield so they could see where to drive.

Verl was in Berlin as it fell. His unit went into the office of Joseph Goebbels, who was the Reich Minister of Propaganda. He took a stack of annotated photographs and a pistol (now lost). The photographs (shown here) appear to each be making a point that Goebbels wanted to "advertise" to the German public, and perhaps others.

Verl Luzena's Photos from Goebbels' Propaganda Office after German Surrender

Dated August 20, 1942, the photo above shows Belgrade, Yugoslavia, which Germany had bombed, invaded, and occupied in April of 1941. Hitler called it "Operation Punishment." The label on the back reads: *A gate of fresh greens decorates the drive.*

Dated April 13, 1944, the label on the back of the photo above reads, roughly: Generalfeldermarschall von Hundstedt at the border of France, reviewing equipment details to consolidate the defense.

The May 25, 1944 label on the back of the photo at left reads, roughly: Generalfeldermarschall von Rundstedt signing the visitors' book at the Soldiers Hospital as staff members proudly look on. (Fontenay, France)

Later in Berlin, Verl sold cigarettes to the Germans. He remembers collecting cigarettes from other GIs, keeping a record of the number of cigarettes each one gave him, then paying the GIs after selling the cigarettes. If he was paid in Russian currency, he'd mark the price up, Then he'd have to go into the Russian zone and find an officer to exchange it. Sometimes when he went into the Russian zone at night, the Russian officers would say, "You got here too late. The girls are all gone!" They meant that the girls they'd had there for their entertainment had left. That wasn't why Verl and his buddies went there, though. Later, after discharge and back home, he bought his first car with his cigarette money.

After V-E Day

When the war ended, Verl worked on an unusual assignment from Eisenhower: to reconnoiter locations where battle-weary troops could be sent for R-and-R. He had a pass signed by Ike and traveled about, getting into touchy situations.

Verl at left with his CCU buddies

Happy Occasions after the War

One fellow in Verl's unit—Art—was about to marry a French woman. His CCU buddies were at an airfield in Germany, and dying to go to the wedding. They asked the CO, who said yes. Since the only plane was out of commission and there were no mechanics, he figured they'd never get it off the ground. But they did, with the bomb bay full of champagne. Verl and a few others made a 17-minute film of the wedding day.

Verl is in a few scenes with a pencil mustache and smacking chewing gum. Since only the military had vehicles and fuel, the wedding party was all dressed up and riding in open jeeps. Probably the first normal life these people had had in six years! Because Art (Authur Mainzer), the groom, happened, as part of the 4th CCU, to film the liberation of Buchenwald, the wedding film is incidentally preserved as part of the United States Holocaust Memorial Museum.

Verl with his pencil mustache. His friends nicknamed him Louie Avec Barbe (Louie with Beard). "Louie" was short for Luzena.

Verl's friend Art and his French bride

The Duchess Returns from Exile after the War

Another happy story is Verl's filming of the return of Charlotte, Grand Duchess of Luxembourg, to her country after the war. She had been in exile in France, Portugal, Great Britain, and North America. While in Britain, she had made broadcasts to the people of Luxembourg. She returned to Luxembourg in April of 1945.

Someone threw a bouquet while the Duchess was crossing a bridge and knocked her hat off. There with his camera, Verl followed her home to the palace and went right inside while she ascended the balcony overlooking the multitude of her celebrating countrymen. A delightful follow-up story in 1962: Verl is standing on that bridge telling his 16-year-old son, John, that story. He hears another man his age telling his 16-year-old son the same story, except it was that man's sister who had thrown that bouquet in 1945. That man was Robert Dolibois, a native Luxembourger, who was their tour director on a Miami University Alumni trip, as he was then the University Alumni Director. He later served as U.S. Ambassador to Luxembourg under President Ronald Reagan. Small world. Or maybe large world with delightful close connections.

Back Home After the War

Verl went back to Miami University to finish his last year and earn his degree in chemistry when he left the Army in 1945. He worked in Connecticut and New York State for E.I. DuPont de Nemours & Co., Inc. He began as a chemist, in time rising up in the ranks to become assistant plant manager. The plant made coated plastics and seat covers. Verl also invented an upholstery material called Jeweltone, using aluminum compounds. His invention was used in many interior decorating fabrics. The company secured a patent for Jeweltone (see NY Times article nearby). Verl was told by his manager, "You've made more money for us with this invention than the whole plant's production this year."

A New Upholstery Plastic Has Shiny Metallic Finish

Patent for Product of Du Pont Describes Use of Aluminum

By STACY V. JONES
Special to The New York Times.

WASHINGTON, Oct. 12—Guests in the lobby of New York's newest hotel, the Americana, are sitting on a du Pont product that was patented this week. It is a plastic upholstery material with a brilliant metallic finish and is called Jeweltone.

The chairs and lounges in the Americana's public rooms are covered with a gold-colored vinyl reproduction of fine damask of the Queen Anne period. In different colors and patterns, the material has found many other applications in interior decoration, automobile upholstery and bookbinding.

E. I. du Pont de Nemours & Co., Inc., estimates sales of vinyl upholstery with the Jeweltone finish at 15,000,000 square yards a year. The company manufactures the material in its fabrics division plant at Newburgh, N. Y., and has licensed other companies to make and sell it.

Patent 3,057,749, obtained by Verl E. Luzena, discloses that the secret of the fabric's opalescent metallic sheen is the use of aluminum compounds. After many experiments, Mr.

Verl E. Luzena

Luzena attained best results with powdered aluminum and one or more of eight pigments called alumina hydrate lakes.

In 1956, when he first applied for a patent, the finish was introduced to the automobile industry. Later it came into use for hotels and restaurants. A pattern called Starpoint, with embossed stars, was chosen for the seating in the Long Beach,

Continued on Page 10, Column 6

DuPont sold the fabric plant to Stauffer Chemical Company in 1972 and Stauffer transferred Verl to San Francisco. He eventually oversaw maintenance and training in their plants across the U.S. until retirement. The marriage of Verl and Ruth ended, and Verl married Diane Butler in 1980. Shortly thereafter, they retired to Baton Rouge, where he became a Louisiana Master Gardener, helped found the farmers market, developed dozens of neighborhood gardens, worked with the state prison system, served the food bank, worked with Louisiana State University, and traveled to El Salvador to provide composting seminars as a guest of the Environmental Ministry. In 2016, the flood of a century destroyed the couple's home, Diane later passed away, and Verl came to Transylvania County to reside with his son.

A Wife's Memoir of the War Years

Verl's first wife, Ruth Gray Luzena, a primary school teacher who started in one-room schoolhouses and eventually ran her own private school (preschool to 2nd grade) and summer camp, sadly, passed away in 2014, after living the last six years of her life in Transylvania County, N.C. She wrote her memoirs, and below are excerpts from her chapter on the war years.

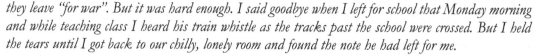

**Ruth and Verl Luzena on
their wedding day**

From Ruth's memoir:

During a war nothing is harder than saying goodbye. The only blessing the first time is knowing that the service requires basic training done in the States and so it isn't as heart-rending as when they leave "for war". But it was hard enough. I said goodbye when I left for school that Monday morning and while teaching class I heard his train whistle as the tracks past the school were crossed. But I held the tears until I got back to our chilly, lonely room and found the note he had left for me.

Mrs. Layer took FDR's request to conserve fuel to the ultimate: we nearly froze all winter and the only time water was hot enough for a bath was when I was in Gettysburg and taking one there as their bathrooms were now finished. Also, she shut off the refrigerator and we kept things on the back porch. Two other teachers rented rooms so at least I had company and we each took one week out of three to do the cooking for all of us. Annetta was a Home Ec teacher and a good cook – but when the other one cooked we all just endured that! We also went out to Gettysburg to have a warm day and a visit, on Saturdays.

Meanwhile, I saved every penny I could to join Verl wherever he was in May, and lived for that day. He had been sent to Colorado for photography school. Then he was sent to California for further basic training and was stationed later in Culver City. On May 3rd, 1943, I boarded the Streamliner in Chicago for Los Angeles, and sat up for three days properly attired in a hat and white gloves—it was the way we dressed, believe it or not.

Verl had gotten a hotel room for us in Hollywood, but to my horror my luggage had been sent on another, slower train and I hadn't a thing but the clothes I had worn on the train for days. But we were scheduled

to go to a USO party that night, and I went, and was duly impressed by the fact that famous movie stars were the entertainers at the USO affairs—Dorothy Lamour was there that night.
My first objective was to get an apartment where I could live and Verl could come to on weekends—easier said than done.

Apartments were so scarce the hotel deskman laughed when I asked where to go. But he didn't know how desperate I was. I got a want ad section and started out. It is positively frightening to look back on how absolutely naïve I was about the entire world!! I didn't realize when I was in a section of town where they opened little peephole doors and told you to go away that I was in the red-light district (didn't know what that was either) or drug dens etc. Wandering back to a degree more respectable area, that is to a very small degree, I saw a sign "For Rent" and went in.

The apartment was a dirty, dingy place with a Murphy bed in the one room wall; the kitchen had a moldy icebox - but it was a place to live for $22 a month, so I took it. My next job after moving in was to find work. That was easier and I got a clerical job in the LA Stock Exchange downtown. This meant walking for an hour both ways through a seedy part of town. I only had my own food rationing book so shopping was difficult and carrying it home not easy.

We were having a great time together as there were USO parties and his photo assignments were often to attend premieres. Seeing movie stars became part of the life: Ronald Reagan was Verl's pay-officer and Alan Ladd was private in Verl's outfit, always standing ahead of him in line so they became friends. Clark Gable was an observer in one of the classes that Verl taught and they were photographed together.

Christmas of 1943 - my first away from home - was dark and gloomy, with no feeling of festivity whatsoever. I had gotten word of Grandpa T's death and was feeling the first pangs of homesickness. But I would soon be back home: Verl was slated to be shipped overseas and our married life together would once again be interrupted. With a heavy heart I quit my job, shipped my things to Oil City and we both headed for Ohio. Verl would go on a fast troop train while I had to take my chances on a low- priority civilian train. It was a five day nightmare.

First of all there were 3000 people waiting to board 28 cars: whoever pushed hardest got on. Once you found a seat you couldn't leave it without having someone to hold it for you and you did the same for them. Most everyone had huge hampers of food as there was only a diner for meals to service men - and perhaps some leftovers for lucky persons. I ate so little during the trip that I lost15pounds.Nor could I sleep as the train stopped at every Podunk Corner and never turned out the lights. In Kansas a kid pulled the emergency brake cord, we came to a lurching halt, and it took hours to get the train moving again. Meanwhile, the pipes all froze, then burst, so you could not use the toilets and dirty water was flooding the cars so we had to hold our feet up in the air.

I was to connect for a train to Ohio in Chicago and because we were late I watched it pull out as we pulled in! In tears by now I sat for 12 hours in the Chicago station in my thin California coat and no boots until my train was ready. But there were vending machines, at last. When Verl caught me as I fell off the train in Gettysburg I was hallucinating and looked dirty and unkempt. I fell into bed at the farm and slept for 24 hours straight. And we only had several days left to be together from his ten days of leave.

Everyone dreaded the Sunday morning that we soon had to face. Verl was due to leave on a very early morning train from Gettysburg. No one said much on the way to the train. I still cannot see a soldier getting on a train and saying goodbye even in a movie without that lump in my throat and my eyes tearing. I also will never forget the heartbreak of the final moment. Verl never looked more handsome than when in his uniform at the height of his young years.

At the moment I had to say goodbye for what could have been forever. It was the very first time I had seen him kiss his mother and hug his father, and I could imagine their feelings as well as my own. During the 50 year D-Day celebrations on TV several years ago I literally OD'd on nostalgia: seeing soldiers boarding trains and kissing goodbye, fields of crosses and all the memories of the war were overwhelming to me. When a Glenn Miller song was played I just broke into sobs all alone on the couch. I cannot speak for Verl as I know little of what the years over there were to him: perhaps the video will be made and he can express some of it himself.

Verl and Ruth in 1943

So Verl headed for New York City and I went back to Oil City. We were still living in the Third St. house but the bank had warned us they wanted to sell it and we should be looking for another place to rent. Although Verl and I had said goodbye thinking it was the last one, we had an unexpected bonus. He called me soon after I got home to say their departure was to be delayed and I should come to NYC and stay until he left. I was ready and called a taxi for the Moonlighter and ran down the front steps of Third St. for the last time, although I did not know that then. There was only one thing on my mind: get to NYC.

Verl had gotten a room in The Taft near Penn Station; our room was on the 18th floor and cost $5 per night. I will let imagination take over in trying to explain what that week was: the first honeymoon plus. You had to think of it as the best week of your life - and the worst, because Verl had no idea how many days he had. Each night I would sit in the room with my heart in my throat listening for his knock - he could never tell me if he was not coming, of course. He wouldn't know until they were put in quarantine. When the knock came we were able to abandon all thought but that we had another 12 hours together.

During the day I was fortunate to have one of Verl's buddy's wife to show me around as they were residents of the city. She took me to every museum and art gallery in town and great places for lunch. In the evening the men would come to the hotel to eat and dance (and pick up girls if there alone). One evening Verl came to the room and said for me to put my best dress on as we were invited to Tom King's brother's for dinner. I was dismayed, wanting to be alone with Verl and picturing a kitchen table with beans and hotdogs or the like. Never was I more wrong: it was an evening to remember. We went to the Hunt Club as his guests (no prices on the menu) and then dancing. Tom was very handsome, and he and Verl were in the same unit throughout their duty, getting together again many times in later years as well.

The Family

Verl and Ruth had two children, John and Diane, who grew up in New Windsor and Cornwall—small villages on the Hudson River just around the bend from West Point. John now lives in Pisgah Forest, N.C., and Diane lives in the small town of Wrightwood in the mountains outside of Los Angeles. Altogether with Verl's stepchildren, Layne and Donna, Verl has six grandchildren and seven great-grandchildren (and counting).

This story was written by Verl Luzena's son, John Luzena.

**Verl Luzena at left, told his stories to his son, John Luzena (seated, center) and Curators
Emmett Casciato (standing) and Tom Bugala (far right)
of the Veterans History Museum of the Carolinas, in June, 2019**

Lawrence Hoffman, U.S. Army

PFC Lawrence Hoffman, age 18

Larry Hoffman was drafted into the Army in 1943 and served in France, Belgium, and Germany. He was discharged in 1946.

I Wanted to Fight the Nazis

Lawrence Hoffman was born in Brooklyn, New York. He remembered, "We moved to the Bronx, and that's where I was when I went into the Army in 1943. I was eighteen. I was given the choice to go to Europe or to the Pacific. I said, 'I want kill Germans.' I joined the Army because the Nazis were killing Jews. I'm a Jew, so I wanted to fight the Nazis.

"After training in New Jersey and Ft. Bragg, I went to Boston to be shipped to England. But before we left, we loaded bombs onto the ship—that was a new one for me! It was a converted cruise ship. I believe it was named, 'The American'. There were 3000 of us soldiers going over.

"I remember once when I was lying on my bunk in the bottom of the ship, this person walked in, I looked up, and he was my cousin. Amazing, isn't it, that we should be on the same ship? We enjoyed ourselves. After that, he went to England and I went to France."

Storming the Beach

"It took us five days to get across the Atlantic, and we landed in Liverpool. From there, I went south to Plymouth, then on another ship to get to the area of the invasion. We didn't land in Normandy until the sixth day after D-Day, because there were 1000 other ships going in there. It was an amazing sight. All those ships and so many balloons overhead. The balloons were there so nobody could dive-bomb us. There was a lot of steel that the Germans had put on the ocean floor, so you couldn't land a boat. The frogmen had to clear it.

"Our ship came in and then we got down in the small boats—the ones you see in the pictures. And we waded ashore and walked up on the beach." Asked what that felt like, Hoffman laughed and said, "We're here and we're gonna stay. It was a nice feeling when you were able to advance. The Germans had their pillboxes—the line, they called it. But there were a lot of people dead. I was in the artillery. We had tremendous casualties that day. A lot of deaths. That's war. That's what it's all about. But the main thing was winning."

Asked if he was afraid, Hoffman said, "You're always afraid. Everybody's afraid. But there's a job to do and we have to do it. And that overcomes your fear. The Nazis killed a lot of Jewish people, and I wanted to get my share as a Jew. Show 'em what it feels like."

Pushing Into France and Belgium

"We went into France, and the Air Force did a thousand-plane bombing that day. It started at 4:00 in the morning and ended at night. And that was the break that we needed to get into France. We landed on the beach and fought our way up to around Saint-Lo. From there, we went south to Brest. People don't remember that, but it was necessary to go to Brest to unload all the equipment that was needed to fight the war.

"After Brest, we started going up to Belgium. We got to Saint Vith, Belgium, on a Friday night. Around 7:00, the Bulge started, and we were forced all the way back to France. And then we turned around and started back up."

Germany and the End of the War

"We went into Germany and went south to Koblenz. There was a tremendous winery there, underground. It ran for about a mile with wine, so we had a good time.

"All the way through Germany to Munich, or Munchen, as they said, and the war ended. I had been in five battles. We would load up, shoot, and then our advisor would tell us when to stop and then move, and start shooting again. The Germans didn't know what to do when they saw us. They were afraid. They would hide. They couldn't believe that the United States had invaded Germany.

**Right: Hoffman with 4.5 artillery gun
in France or Belgium**

"After the war ended, we went into some German towns. I could understand a little bit of what they said. Jewish is a little bit like German, especially in the northern end. You could communicate a little bit. And some of them spoke some English. They were surprised. They didn't realize there were Jewish soldiers in the American Army.

"The German people said they didn't know anything about what the Nazis were doing. But that was a lot of baloney. They knew all about it. They knew about the concentration camps. There were so many camps. People worked there. They cooked and worked in the camps. Word must have spread. They knew."

Concentration Camps Freed

"We freed a couple of camps. The camps were surrounded by a fence. There were maybe 50 or 60 people in each house. The people came out—they were just skin and bones, bones sticking out. The Nazis had made them work—work in the fields—and they had died in the fields. Those left were so sick and hungry, they couldn't even walk. We gave them MREs to eat, then we set up our cooking equipment and cooked a hot meal for them. They were so happy to see us. Don't forget, these were people that were taken from all these countries and put into the camps. Now they were free to go home, to see their own people. I don't know exactly what happened next, because we would free the camp and move on.

"The German guards had fled. They knew the war was over. They weren't going to be captured by us, so they took off."

Back Home in New York

"To go home after the war, I got on a ship in Belgium. It was a small ship that took months; a lot of people were sick. When I came back to New York, I took a train, then a taxi to get home. When I was walking down the street toward my house in the Bronx, I looked up and there was my father. I yelled at him, 'Hey. Dad!' Back at the house, I went upstairs, there was my mother, and she was overjoyed. That was it.

"I was discharged January 6, 1946. After that, I became a policeman. I did 21 years as a New York City policeman—enjoyed every minute of it. I liked doing something to help people. What patrolmen do, is to help when there's an accident, get medical help, notify parents, go in to help families. People think a cop is just going to lock you up or chase you down the street. But we do so much to help.

"From World War I, so many from my family have been in the service. My uncle was wounded in World War I, my brothers and I were in World War II, my cousins were in World War II. My son-in-law and grandchild were in the Marines, serving in Afghanistan and other places. So war seems to be a thing in our family.

Family Life

Larry and Ann Annunziata met in the Bronx, N.Y., were married in 1948, and have two daughters, Janice and Debra. Larry and Ann live in Brevard and Ormond Beach, Florida. Over the years, they have enjoyed spending time with their family, traveling, boating, and fishing.

Larry and Ann Hoffman

Larry Hoffman in 2019 at the Veterans History Museum of the Carolinas, remembering D-Day, 1944

SSgt. Ray J. Norris I, U.S. Army

SSgt. Ray Norris I, U.S. Army 656th Tank Destroyer Battalion, Medical Detachment Company, serving in England, France, and Germany.
He entered the Army in March 1943 and was discharged in August 1945.

A Story of a Father and Son in Two Wars, by Ray Norris II

My Father Raymond J. Norris I was born in June 1906 and I, his son Raymond J. Norris II, was born in July 1945. This is the story of our journeys and service in World War II and the Vietnam War.

Part I: Father

Ray J. Norris I was working in Toledo, Ohio when he was drafted into the U.S. Army on March 15, 1943 (37 years old) and was assigned to Camp Perry, Ohio. Later he was sent to Camp Hood, Texas to prepare for leaving for combat in World War II. It was during this time that he met my mother, Margaret Monica Ehly, a farm girl who was working as a volunteer at USO. SSgt Norris and Ms. Ehly were married on May 1, 1944 in Lampasas, Texas in St. Mary's Church. He left for Service outside the Continental US on Dec 16, 1944. burkh

The history below was compiled by Robert F. Jackson, 1st Lt. Inf (TD),
Acting Adjutant 656th Tank Destroyer Battalion APO 403.

SSgt Norris was assigned to the 656th Tank Destroyer Battalion in the Medical Detachment Company. The unit, commanded by LTC John Meador, landed in England on the last day of December 1944. It remained on the southern coast of England for almost a month. The unit moved across the English Channel in LSTs to France. From this camp the battalion marched across France and Belgium to the vicinity of Liege where it joined the 9th Armored Division.

On the 28th of February 1945 the battalion moved through Aachen, Germany and crossed the Roer River near Duren. Then as part of the armored spearhead, it fought east to Romagen and the Rhine River. On the 7th of March 1945 when the Ladendorf Bridge was captured intact by First Army troops, "destroyer" from Company "C" were the first Tank Destroyers to cross the Rhine River into the bridgehead. The entire battalion crossed over to the east side of the Rhine River and occupied direct fire positions during the expansion of the bridgehead.

When the First Army broke out of the Romagon Bridgehead, the battalion rolled southeast to Limburg, then turned and raced north to Warburg, taking in stride all of the resistance it met. A short rest, and the long march on Loipzig began. The battalion pushed far east as the Muldo River where units from the 69th Division took over and went on to meet the Russians.

After the Yanks and the Russians met, the battalion was assigned to the Third Army. It then moved to Weiden, near the Czechoslovakian border. A week or two later the unit moved to Bayrouth, Germany where it began preparations for the return home.

Raymond J. Norris I left Europe on June 23, 1945 returned to Camp Hood, Texas on July 2, 1945, in time to see Raymond J. Norris II born at McCloskey General Hospital in Temple Texas.

After discharge from the Army on August 31, 1945, the family moved back to Toledo, Ohio where we all made a home in South Toledo. My father Raymond J Norris I died in May, 1958, and my mother passed in August, 1972.

Part II: Son

Raymond (now also known as Ray) J Norris II (I dropped the II after my father passed) grew up in Toledo Ohio. I went to Immaculate Conception Catholic Elementary School, St Francis De Sales Catholic High School and The University of Toledo where I graduated with a Bachelor of Science in Civil Engineering.

During the short time I got to spend with my father, he did talk about his time in World War II and his experiences in Europe. He never talked about this time in his life with my mother that I was aware of. My dad did share two particular "words of wisdom" with me during our talks while he ran a small appliance repair business in the attic of our home.

He said, "Son, if you ever have to go into the army, go as an officer, as it is always easier telling someone where to dig the hole than it ever is digging the hole." The second bit of advice he gave me was to be kind and respectful of the enlisted men you command as it is those men that will bring you through as an officer." I took his advice on both items of guidance.

Little did my father know that the war in Viet Nam would become very active when I was at the University of Toledo. I entered the ROTC Program (remembering my father's advice) and when I graduated, I was commissioned as a Second Lieutenant in June 1968.

I entered active duty in the US Army on September 16, 1968, and was assigned to Fort Belvoir in Alexandria, Virginia to begin Engineer Officers Training. Upon my completion of this training, I was assigned to Ft. Riley in Junction City, Kansas to a Combat Engineer Battalion there in preparation for duty in Viet Nam.

I left for Viet Nam on August 24, 1969, assigned to the 27th Combat Engineer (Tiger) Battalion [18th Engineer Brigade, 45th Engineer Group] and was promoted to 1LT on September 16, 1969. This Combat Engineer Battalion took up operations in the I Corps Tactical Zone at Gia Le.

Our base camp was at Camp Eagle (101st Airborne) near Phu Bai and Hue, Viet Nam. I was initially assigned to be Platoon Leader in Company D at FSB Birmingham. Four months later I was assigned to the S-3 section of the Engineer Battalion since I was one of two civil engineers in the entire unit.

At right, Ray J. Norris II

The basic charge of the battalion was to build Route 547 from Phu Bai to the A Shau Valley. My platoon unit camped at FSB (Fire Support Base) Birmingham, FSB Bastogne, and FSB Blaze. Each time we moved to a new FSB the artillery shelled the new location, the infantry would secure the site, and then our engineer unit (men and heavy equipment) would be airlifted to the site.

We would then dig in bunkers set up perimeters with towers and barbed wire. Since the artillery usually followed us to the new site, we would build gun pads for the howitzers who would fire around 200 rounds into the A Shau Valley every night. The camp was frequently mortared at night, so we were glad to have protected bunkers.

We would build a tracer road down from the new site to the planned area for the extension of Route 547. As we built each new section of road, our unit would then do mine-sweeping operations every morning. For the most part "Charlie" (the enemy) would leave us alone while we were building the roads and bridges as they used these at night.

We always flew the large red engineer flag with the castle on all vehicles signifying we were the "engineers." It usually worked well.

112

After I was assigned as the S-3, I developed a design team which put together a "engineer plan of action" for each unit in our battalion. I would then get a helicopter ride each day to deliver the plans to all of the outlying camps we were responsible for and meet with each officer to discuss the civil engineering plans for their unit.

One time when I went to visit the engineer unit at FSB T-Bone, they were under an active attack by "Charlie" in the middle of the day. Needless to say, I was glad to get back to base camp at Phu Bai that evening.

While I was in Nam, my son Douglas (with his dad in photo at right) was born in November, 1969. I received many pictures of my son while I was in-country, but I did not get to see him until I returned to Toledo in August of 1970. It was a great and very happy experience for me to see him for the first time.

A second great experience for me was being award the Bronze Star (shown at right) for achievement while I was ending my tour in Nam. I just recently found out my father was awarded two Bronze stars during his tour with the 656th Tank Destroyers in World War II. Dad never talked about those medals with me when he told me about his experiences, however it gave me great pride about my father.

One last item of related military association in my family: My daughter Kimberlie Kay (Norris) England (who was born in May 1973) is married to Colonel John Wojcik, a JAG officer in the Michigan National Guard based out of Lansing Michigan. He just recently celebrated 30 years in the service. Kimberlie enjoys the military side of her life.

Kimberlie introduced me to my wife Barbara on July 4, 2003 and we were married on the first day of spring, May 20, 2004. We came down to Brevard to visit some friends and fell in love with the people here and the area. We built and moved into our dream home in Eagle Lake on November 15, 2006. It overlooked the Blue Ridge Parkway and the Pisgah National Forest with great sunsets. While we loved this area and the folks at Eagle Lake (still do), we moved "off the mountain" and down to the city on November 9th, 2015.

Barb and I (pictured at right) still travel around the country with our dog Winston. We have camped in 42 states and been to 23 National Parks. We also enjoy very much the people here in Brevard and our extended family at Sacred Heart Parish.

Life gives us many experiences to build on, but two of them were my discussions with my father about his experiences in World War II and my "young man growing up" happenings from Viet Nam. Not only the civil engineering events but the men (enlisted and other officers) I met along the way. I used those work and people skills I learned in my 31 years for the City of Toledo and for a private architect/engineer in Toledo as a civil engineer for 9 years. They all helped bring us to the wonderful city of Brevard, North Carolina.

PFC George Burkhart, U.S. Army

PFC George Burkhart, U. S. Army, European Theatre

George Burkhart served in the U.S. Army Infantry from 1944-1945,
surviving time in a German Stalag (prisoner of war camp).

By Carl Burkhart

George was thirty-seven years old when he went to prison. But that was okay…it meant that he was probably coming home. The prison's name was Stalag 12B.

A few months before his incarceration, although I was only four years old I remember looking out of the bay window of our second-floor apartment as George—"Pop" to me—walked down the street in his uniform—he was off to war. Mom was with me, softly crying, her cheek next to mine.

The strange part of the situation was the fact that Pop had been serving in uniform when he was drafted. He was a member of the Coast Guard's Volunteer Port Security Force, doing dockside patrol duty a couple of nights a week after work wearing the uniform of a bos'ns mate. In spite of that, he was still eligible for the draft!

As I grew up, watching my kind, humble Pop grow old I often tried to picture him on his belly crawling across France with an M1 rifle cradled in his arms. Not possible.

Yet it happened.

I tried to picture him aiming his rifle at another human being and pulling the trigger. Absolutely impossible! Not this man who sang tenor every Sunday in the choir, who jumped up from the table to get you more ice for your drink, who was a clerk for an insurance company.

Yet it happened.

Watching the movie "Stalag 17" the other night, I tried to picture Pop in that barrack. Not easy.

Yet it happened.

I have a V-mail letter Pop had written home while in a field hospital shortly after his liberation from the Stalag. He had adopted a little family of body lice in the Stalag, hence the hospitalization for delousing as well as nourishment and other treatment.

He was well into his eighties before I got him to speak of his service in the Army of the United States. I have discovered that this is common in those who have experienced battle face-to-face. He still didn't say much. He told me that after he was drafted they pulled a bunch of his back teeth that were in bad shape. "There are no dentists where you're going…," they told him. Kindly, the army had fitted him with false teeth—which he wore for the remaining fifty years of his life.

Pop didn't say much about the Stalag. He spoke a little German with the guards, who apparently didn't want to be there either. Being of German descent, I imagine he felt a certain affinity for his captors. I can't imagine him *hating* another human being.

He had been wounded—a nick in the arm and another in the ear. I have imagined with horror the possibility of the trajectory of those bullets going a few inches to the right or to the left. My brother, born ten years after the War, may have had similar thoughts.

War. They took an insurance clerk, yanked his teeth out, gave him an M-1, and told him to go shoot at his ethnic brothers. Pop got his ticket to the Stalag by surrendering…under what circumstances, I don't know. But I'm glad he surrendered. He's a hero to me.

"WE SHALL COME HOME VICTORIOUS."

Charles Dickson, 82nd Airborne Paratrooper

D-Day Paratrooper Charles Dickson, U.S. Army

Charles Dickson joined the U.S. Army in December, 1943. In the 82nd Airborne, he jumped into Sainte-Mère-Église on D-Day. He retired from the Army in 1966 as a Master Sergeant.

I'd Rather Fight On Somebody Else's Land Than Mine

Charles Dickson remembers: "I went into service in December 1943. I wasn't drafted, I joined. I joined because the world—we needed to get rid of somebody. It was our country. You ought to protect it. If England had got captured, then it would have been hell. I'd rather fight on somebody else's land than mine. You can fight on their land, tear it up, and then come home."

Fifty Dollars a Month to Jump Out of Airplanes

"After basic training, I was a private making $21.00 a month. By the time they took the $6.40 a month for insurance, etc., I didn't have but $12.00 a month to spend. Then all of a sudden it happened they were starting a jump school and they were paying $50.00 a month to jump out of airplanes. So I decided if I was going to get killed, I might as well die with money in my pocket. So I went to jump school and graduated from there and went to Ft. Bragg.

"In April of '44, I walked in and the captain said, 'Private, are you prepared to go overseas?' I said, 'No, sir.' He said, 'Well, you got three days to get ready to go.' So I left there in six days.

PFC Charles Dickson at Jump School, Fort Benning, Alabama-Georgia

We Were in the First Group to Go Into Normandy

"So I went to Northern Scotland and joined the 82nd Airborne up there. Then we went down to Leicester in England. There were 800 planes with 20 men in each plane. We got prepared and loaded up on June 5 and left in the night. I remember we were in clouds. It was radio silence. All eight hundred planes that went over were radio silence. They couldn't see pea turkey. We were in the first group to go into Normandy. They all didn't go in at once. I think the next group went in two hours later.

"They put us up at fifteen hundred feet because the Germans had those sausage balloons up there with the cables hanging down. If you were under that, you could run into them. Lot of the pilots got gun fever and were getting too fast. If you jump out at 125 miles an hour, you would rupture. So you try to come in at 110-115, and get out. But in war, nobody's sitting there with a damn speedometer.

Downed German aircraft

"Most of us had 70-80 pounds, according to what your weight was. I weighed 170—you could be a total of 200—so I had a load. It was K-rations or extra ammunition—50 rounds. Or grenades—things that you would need. They'd put you maybe six hand grenades—that would put a weight on you. It was heavy. It makes you fall faster, too. And I had a Thompson sub-machine gun. They had those and little carbines with collapsible butts. You could slide 'em in and pull 'em out and they were small. You couldn't have a big M-1 or B.A.R.

"If you're smart and can see the ground, you reach up and pull your chute. Sort of like getting off an escalator. But if you miss it, you shook all the fillings out of your damn teeth.

"They were the old chutes. You could be in a half thing and if that son-of-a-bitch opened, it would jerk your butt plumb up to the top. If the leg things weren't tight, shit, it would wear a blister on you. But if you were lucky and you went out and your feet came out, it opened up there instead of in a half-thing.

"The morning before, I understand, they went over and dropped simulated parachutists. That was to throw them [the Germans] off, that they were going to be there. When the Germans found out that they were dummies, they thought, 'Oh, they're just trying to draw us off.' That was a decoy."

D-Day

"Eisenhower called it. He said we'd go on the sixth because we'd had bad weather in the [English] Channel before. They said, 'You got two days of operational weather.' He said, 'That's it.' And it was right, because it did rain and pour like you don't believe after that. If they'd picked the wrong day, we couldn't go. You get a wet chute, that's just a springer and down you go. You don't want that. They had us sit there for two days—we didn't know when we were going to go. We didn't know it was because of the weather. The good part about it—the less you know, the better. I know Patton used to have news conferences, but he would only have one person come in there and Patton told him what he wanted him to know. That person went back and dispersed the information. It's not like today when a whole bunch go in there.

"You know that rock [Pointe-du-Hoc] on Normandy Beach—they sent the Rangers up on it—they didn't have any damn guns up there. They just had ropes.

"We flew in clouds I don't know how long, but all of a sudden they flipped the yellow light on and I remember it was 2:22 in the morning. I got up and hitched up and looked out, and the only thing I could see was the glow off the C-47 exhaust.

Clicking That Little Buster Brown Clicker

"And I jumped. And I didn't know whether I was going to get barbed-wire fence, pine trees, or what. But I hit the ground in a pasture or something like that. It wasn't woods. See if you could see a light or something. You just didn't know where you were. You were sitting there. And I had my little clicker, so I clicked around. Buster Brown clicker. If you heard something, you clicked. If somebody clicked back, he'd say, 'Where are you?' and I'd say, 'Over here.' Then somebody would join up. We just sort of got together. If they didn't click back, we'd just pull the damn trigger.

"One of the guys got hung up on the steeple of a church. And he just hung up there. The Germans came by and thought he was dead—he just lay still. And finally, we went in and got him. But he was hanging on the side of that church for half a day.

"I guess when you're eighteen, you don't believe cow horns hook. You just get right in the middle of it. This was everybody. You didn't have time to be afraid. You had to be on your alert trying to protect your ass. I kept my damn finger on the trigger."

Street Fighting and Protecting the Bridge in Sainte-Mère-Église

"So that was it. And then when we got daylight, we began to gather in groups of two or three. I was in H Company, and I think there were eight or ten of us together, and with other outfits. So we found a road that we needed to go to Sainte-Mère-Église, to the bridge, protect the bridge—keep it from being blown up—so we got that. And I think maybe the second day, the Germans came up the road, and they had three great big Royal Tiger tanks coming up the road. We didn't have anything except bazookas.

"But there was two little corporals

on the side of that hill, and they stood up and popped the first one with a bazooka—knocked him right out in the middle of the road—dead. But they went down and they knocked all three of those Tiger tanks out. They got the Congressional Medal of Honor. I don't know their names or anything, but I saw them do it.

German Tiger Tank
Dickson: "We fought them on day two of D-Day."

"And so we had some street fighting and all, and we captured Sainte-Mère-Église. We held that, and then the 101st took Saint-Lô. So we had them locked in. We weren't there but three weeks, and they took us back to England because we were so shot up. There were less than 9,000 of us left of the two divisions.

"I had twisted my shoulder—dislocated on the jump—so they put me on med for two or three weeks and got it straightened up. Then we made the Southern France invasion in Aix-en-Provence and went in, in gliders. We went in behind lines to protect the railroads, so they [Germans] couldn't bring anything in through Marseille. That was the last time and only time I ever rode a glider.

"We went in and it looked so pretty and green. As we got maybe a thousand yards away from landing, the pilot just peeled off to the right. We went down beside the trees and they knocked the wings off. I don't remember when we got on the ground. What it was, was a grape vineyard planted by the Romans. They were bigger than forty or 50 inches around.

"The other gliders coming in would hit those and cartwheel. We killed more men than the Germans did. And that was the last time gliders were ever used. They would've had to tie me in, to get me in another one."

Pushing Into the French Alps

"We went up the Rhone River to the little town, Nancy, France. I remember it because my sister's name was Nancy. They issued us winter clothing. Now this was October. We were fixing to get in the French Alps. It was heavy winter clothes, and we went in, and it was just like the Blue Ridge here. You go up one mountain and there would be another behind it. It wasn't any roads, it was just paths going over. This was in Southern France in the Colmar Pocket.

Charles Dickson

"I got leave and went to Paris for Thanksgiving. I went to Notre Dame Cathedral then. I got back and we had captured part of the Maginot Line, the French line. It was two and three storeys underneath. I said, 'Oh, God, we'll be here all winter, underground, have to dig, and we're just getting settled in for the winter.'"

The Battle of the Bulge

"On December 17, we got orders to move out. We loaded up on deuce-and-a-half-trucks and went to Metz, France, which was about two hundred miles. We got there and we needed gas, and we didn't have it. It had been given to Montgomery up north. We hit the ground walking and we walked a hundred miles in fifty hours, in snow up to your butt. We got to Bastogne and fought for three days and freed it. Then me and three other of my men went behind lines to see what was going on behind there. The ground was frozen, and snow, and we found a cemetery. And they had mausoleums. The dead people didn't need 'em as bad as we did. We used the mausoleums to burn coffins and bones to keep warm.

"We stayed there for two weeks, then went back to the lines. We reported every night at 11:00 by radio to tell them what was going on. Then they called us back and opened a front a day before the Germans were ready. Patton jumped the gun. This was around Bastogne, the Battle of the Bulge.

"We'd come down with yellow jaundice, so they put us in the hospital for two or three weeks. We got rid of lice, got to sleep on sheets. There was a big, tall nurse come in there one day and says, 'Are you about ready to go?' I said, 'Oh, I'm never going to leave here. I'm not going to make it.' She says, 'What in the hell are you talking about?' I said, 'I haven't slept on a damn sheet in a year or two. And I'll be damn if I'm going to leave these white sheets for a damn foxhole.'"

Pushing Into Germany

"But then we started on the drive and went to the Rhineland, and crossed the Rhine River at Ludwigshafen and Mannheim. And we got hold of the autobahn. I'll never forget, I went into Heidelberg, and it was an open city. The Germans had agreed not to fire or anything.

"The next battle was Heilbronn. That was the home of the SS, sort of like our West Point. Now that was a damn street fight. It was kids ten, twelve, fourteen years old, sitting in doorways with guns. If you brought a Jeep down, they'd just pop your ass right there. So we got smart and started blowing holes in the walls of one room of the house instead of going out in the open. So we hit the autobahn and went all the way to Linz, Austria. That's where we met the Russians. And that was the end of the battles.

"I was fortunate, I didn't get any major wounds. You know, you got hit with shrapnel. A piece went in my leg, a medic pulled it out, put two or three stitches in it, and you didn't go back [to the field hospital]. That was too far to walk."

Prisoner liberated at Dachau Concentration Camp, April, 1945

After V-E Day

"So then, after the war, I was stationed in Stuttgart. I didn't realize it at the time, but I got a really good sight of Europe then. The first thing we did, we were bringing back machinery from the Alps—out of the mountains of Germany. The Germans had stored it there. They thought the French might capture it and take it back to France. We had deuce-and-a-half trucks. We would go back to the barns and load it to take it back to Stuttgart.

"When you go over there—I think of Stuttgart because I stayed there the most—it's a beautiful big town. I mean it had six hills—you know, like Rome's got seven hills. By the time we got through cleaning up all the mess, we had seven hills. The big bahnhof railroad—God-amighty, it'd make Grand Central Station—it was beautiful—I saw pictures of it before and after it was bombed. And the towns and all, just ruptured.

Hitler's home in Munich

Coming down the Rhine River, I saw a jewelry center prior to the war, and they turned it into a ball bearing plant. It was two creeks coming right down the middle of it, and there was a church sitting right in the middle of it. There were houses, and they had crosses on those houses, just like in the Bible where they put names.

"The Eighth Air Force had stopped there for a thousand-plane raid and they unloaded on it. You couldn't even drive a Jeep through it—it was totally demolished. And yet down the river, there was a damn big aircraft plant underground. The Air Force came and they bombed like hell. They didn't even slow down those fifteen thousand workers they had there. They were building those Messerschmitts—the jets. It was underground. Concrete was the secret of the success of Germany.

"They had tunnels and all—you could bomb all damn day and you wouldn't even bother them. And the only way we got through the Maginot Line is the Siegfried Line. They had air ducts at the top. You could sit there and a five-inch gun would come up out of the ground: ch-ch-ch-ch-ch, and go back down. You could sit there with a 155 and it would ricochet just like a .22 off of it. We'd open up, machine guns and engineers, we'd go up on the top of the thing and get at the air ducts. We'd drop that damn composition C down the damn air thing, light it, and run like hell and it would blow up. That's the way we broke through the Maginot Line."

The Germans' Underground Trains

"They had trains under there. Hell, they two and three storeys of trains. There's a little town of Bitche that had never been captured since the Thirty-year War. The Maginot Line and the Siegfried Line were about twenty miles apart. Bitche was sitting in no-man's-land between the two. They had the dragon teeth concrete—you couldn't get a tank over it. You could blow it up with dynamite, but you had to do it the hard way.

"The next job I got was restoring a Coca-Cola plant in Bad Cannstatt, Germany. That was the premium of all. And we served Coca-Colas on July the Fourth, '45. That was the best morale-builder there had ever been, because we nobody had tasted a Coke in all this time. So I was over there, and I figured I was a country boy, I'd probably never have money enough to come back over here, and I'm not going home right now. I'm going to stay over here and look at things, so I got to be in the headquarters of the Seventh Army there."

General Patton

"General Patton had taken over. I remember one morning we were going down the street, and there was an old lady sitting on the side of the road with a hatchet cutting concrete off of bricks, to rebuild them. She could whistle—God a-mighty, you could hear it for miles. She whistled one day and we went over there to see. She said, 'We've got to have bread. They're rationing flour.'

"General Patton said, 'Open up the damn bakeries—no more rationing of food.' The people could go get bread. That's why Germany did so well after the war—Patton let them do the way they were accustomed to doing. Patton let them run the country the way that they were most happy with. That's why we were successful. I was in a car behind him when they had the wreck near Heidelberg. No window broke or a thing—no crash, or anything. It was just shock and it snapped a vertebra in his neck, and he was paralyzed from there down. He died December 20, 1945, of pneumonia."

Running the U.S.O.

"I stayed over there. I got to run the U.S.O. The most famous ones I had were George Burns and Larry Adler. Adler was a harmonicist. I took him behind lines in France to the harmonica plant, where he could get some new harmonicas. They gave me a box of little one-inch harmonicas. And they had Martha Tilton, Edgar Bergen, Jo Stafford, Bob Crosby. That was it, and I decided I believed it was time for me to come home."

Charles Dickson's Medals

Dickson in 2019

"I came back into Ft. Bragg in April, got four years of G.I. Bill. I've had no desire to go back. I've seen it once. It's sort of like Satchel Page said, 'Don't look back, they might be gaining on you.'"

**Charles Dickson in 2019
with his WWII photo**

John J. McCarthy, U.S. Coast Guard

Chief Petty Officer John J. McCarthy, U.S. Coast Guard

*John McCarthy served in the Coast Guard before and during World War II. When the war started, he was based in San Juan, Puerto Rico. He was reassigned to the cutter **Unalga** for convoy duty on the East Cost, where German U-Boats had sunk many merchant ships. When the war in the Pacific ended, he helped bring American troops home from the Philippines and Hawaii, serving on the attack transport* **Joseph P. Dickman.**

Veterans History Museum of the Carolinas volunteer Michael McCarthy recorded his father's story of convoy duty during WWII, when the Coast Guard was under Navy command.

137

John McCarthy told his story in 2014:

"When I joined the Coast Guard it was a commitment for three years. Navy was four and the Coast Guard was three. We went on board a ship [*The Northland*] and they just trained us on the ship. Mine was a ship that traditionally went up to Alaska and the Bering Sea and the Arctic Ocean—an icebreaker. Every year it made an annual trip and stayed up there all summer.

"We visited Nome, Ketchikan, Juneau and Dutch Harbor. And the Aleutian Islands and Southeastern Alaska. I remember one time I went swimming in the Arctic Ocean with some of my shipmates. We just swam out from our ship. Ice-cold water! We didn't stay in long, we just wanted to say we'd done it.

"Our ship was going to be re-stationed to Oakland, California. They gave us a choice to stay in Seattle or go with the ship. I said, 'Let's go.' I was in Los Angeles/San Pedro for most of the time. We patrolled Alaska during the summer. We were there to help and rescue people in trouble. We went to Dutch Harbor, which was the gateway to the Bering Sea.

"We went to Point Barrow, Alaska, where the great flyer Wiley Post had crashed a plane with Will Rogers his passenger. They were both killed. Going there was a big thrill for a young kid. Our ship, the *Northland*, was going there to carry a monument to the site of that crash. Big and heavy. Marble, probably.

"My three years were up. I'd always wanted to see New York, so I figured this was the time to do it. I took a train to New York, stayed at the YMCA, and saw the sights. Then I went to the recruiting office in New York and, surprise, there was my old warrant officer from Seattle. I re-signed for three more years. They sent me to San Juan, Puerto Rico. That was when the war started.

"My wife-to-be, Laurel Crawford, lived in Jacksonville, Florida. We met when my ship [the *Unalga*] was being refitted in a Jacksonville shipyard [with depth charge launchers for anti-submarine convoy duty].

John, standing, third from left with his Coast Guard buddies

"I went on a ship doing convoy duty in the Caribbean from Port of Spain, Trinidad. That area was easy picking for the U-boats because we weren't quite geared up yet. We escorted tankers and merchant ships.

"A typical convoy would be thirty to forty merchant ships. We'd have five escort ships. We had radar and sound equipment to detect the U-boats. If we detected one, we'd drop depth charges on them to try to drive them away or destroy them. Sometimes we didn't really know if we got them. We never had one surface on us; that's how you'd know if you got one.

"Once we had a new officer, a '90 day wonder' as they were called—inexperienced and assigned to sea after only 90 days of training. After we had dropped depth charges on a suspected submarine, he saw bubbles coming to the surface. The officer got excited and yelled, 'She's a-sar-facing!' Of course, it was just bubbles from the depth charge, not the submarine. We laughed behind his back.

"Then I got transferred to a different ship [the corvette *Intensity*], running from New York to Guantanamo Bay, Cuba. I don't remember being too scared. We just figured we'd get them before they got us. I was just a kid. We weren't afraid. We had K-guns and all kinds of stuff to get a U-boat. I was a Bosun's Mate, which was to take care of the deck and maintenance on the ship. On topside, we steered, signaled, and quarter-mastered. We ran the ship.

"I don't think we got much news about what was going on in the war. We didn't have TV or radio. But we had movies. They'd show a movie for recreation for the crew every night. I wasn't much of a movie fan, so I don't remember what the movies were.

The War in Europe Ends

"When Germany surrendered and the war was over in Europe, there was nothing left in the Atlantic for all the escort ships to do. They were laying up all the ships and thousands of people. I got sent to Oakland, California to work on a big attack transport, *The Joseph P. Dickman*. We were about to leave California to head into the South Pacific [for the invasion of Japan] when the Japs surrendered.

"We went to Pearl Harbor several times. I saw *The Arizona*, sunk in the ocean.

"The war was over, but there were tens of thousands of troops all over the world who needed to come home. My ship went to Honolulu, Pearl Harbor, and into the Philippines and picked up thousands of troops—as many as we had bunks for and could feed. It was a long trip back to the U.S. It took a long time, maybe ten days. On that ship we probably made fifteen-sixteen knots.

"We went across the Pacific to Tacoma, Washington and dropped the troops off. We left and went back to the South Pacific and got another load of soldiers. They'd made it through the war and they were going home.
"We tried to entertain them somewhat. On the forward deck a band would play and we had some singers. We unloaded that second load at San Francisco Bay. There was a big Army base there.

"When I left the ship they took the crew off and turned the ship over to the Navy yard. Then they sent everybody back to their home bases, and my registered base was Charleston, South Carolina. That suited me fine because my wife, Laurel, was in Jacksonville, Florida."

John had served in both the Atlantic and Pacific during World War II.

Pictured, Laurel and John McCarthy on their wedding day, June 11, 1944, at St. Michael's Church on 34th Street in New York City.

John and Laurel had three boys (from left), Michael, Patrick, and Jack (pictured below).

Harold Wellington, Merchant Marine, U.S. Army, U.S. Navy

Harold Wellington, U.S. Navy

Harold Wellington served in the Merchant Marine from 1942 to 1946, the U.S. Army in 1948, and the U.S. Navy from 1950 to 1954. He served in Africa, Europe, and the Middle East.

A Young Man in Vermont

Harold Wellington tells his story: "I was living in Brownsville, Vermont. I tried to join the service before the war when I was 17 but my dad wouldn't let me. He wouldn't sign the papers. But when I turned 18 in 1942, I went down to Massachusetts to join the Navy. Back then, they didn't have recruiting offices in every little town, so I had to go across to another state.

"I'd always had my heart set on going into the Navy. Back then, everybody was joining the service. The Navy said, 'We can't take enlistments. We've got too many people. You've gotta go through your draft. And when you go through the draft, they'll put you where they want you—wherever they need you.' I was working on a farm, and farm help was deferred, so they probably wouldn't have drafted me. So I didn't want to go through the draft and be put into the Army. I was working on a farm for $25.00 a month and my keep.

"The Navy wouldn't take me, but I saw this place that had a sign saying 'Join the Merchant Marine.' Being non-educated, right-off-the-farm, all I knew was that they went to sea, and that's what I wanted. I had no idea how it was set up, so I joined the Merchant Marine. They sent me to Brooklyn, New York to boot camp. I didn't realize that the Merchant Marine wasn't classed as a service; it was just a civilian job. But it got you deferred from the draft."

In the Merchant Marine: Traveling to Africa, Europe, and the Middle East

"Boot camp was run by the Coast Guard. All we did was learn military history, protocol, and learned how to abandon ship and row life boats. They sent me aboard ship, showed me where the fire room was and said, 'You are now a fireman and water tender. You'll be here for the next eight hours on duty,' then turned around and walked out. No training, no nothing. I'd never seen a boiler in my life. I had to learn everything all by myself. Nobody showed me anything. I just had to figure it out. This valve does this. This valve does that. You just figure it out after a while. We always traveled in convoys escorted by Naval destroyers and British Corvettes," Harold laughed. "Of course, we were always escorted by the German subs, too.

"First we went to Galveston, Texas, but I don't know how we made it past the North Carolina coast, because they were blowing up ships like crazy down there. My first trip in early '43 was to London while the Germans were bombing England. You could hear them coming. We were taking war supplies to our troops in Europe. Then the next ship I got on, we went to the Mediterranean, down through the Suez Canal, into the Indian Ocean, and over to the Persian Gulf. By that time, the lend-lease supplies to Russia were going by rail because, previously, going by ship to Murmansk, Russia, was a death trap. If half the ships made it there, they were lucky.

"The Army had built a railroad from Iran to Russia, which nobody knew anything about. Or maybe the Germans knew about the railroad, but they were busy somewhere else. So that's where we took the supplies—to Iran. So we could get supplies through to Russia that way. The chance of losing our ships was much smaller going to Iran than to Murmansk."

Left, an American engine transporting Allied aid for Russia, stopping at a station, c.1943 (stock photo)

Right, American and British railroad crews taking supplies from Iran to Russia, c.1943 (stock photo)

"Then I made a second trip to Iran and Iraq and then down the east coast of Africa to South Africa, then back up into the Suez Canal to Italy and North Africa. Our troops had got out of Africa by then and were fighting in Italy. We were picking up armaments from Africa and taking them to Italy or bringing them back to the States.

"We had been in Bari and Taranto, Italy when the rumors of the D-Day invasion came. We were hearing scuttlebutt that it was coming—rumors. We unloaded supplies in Italy and we all held our breath, wondering what we were going to do when we left Italy. Would we go to France for the invasion? But they sent us to North Africa to load up scrap metal. We knew we were on Easy Street then because we knew we wouldn't be taking scrap metal to France. We had been back in New York six days when D-Day came, so we missed it by six days. We were lucky.

"We had a Swedish ocean liner (cruise ship) that had been converted to a troop transport. I made two trips to France on that ship to bring our troops home after the war. They were liberating prisoner of war camps in Germany and we were bringing our troops home. I was an oiler in the engine room. The Army had medical treatment facilities on the ship."

Above right, Swedish ocean liner *M.S. John Erickson,* converted into a troop transport ship, brought American prisoners of war home when World War II ended.

Asked how it felt to be bringing these sick, wounded, and badly treated POWs home, Harold said, "At the time, you were glad, but you don't think much of it. You're just doing your job. But later on in life, you realize what it was. It was just so great.

"I got on a Liberty ship and went to Portugal and France. I was in Marseille, France on V-J [Victory Over Japan] Day. We weren't supposed to go off the ship after 10:00 pm, but we went anyway. We went ashore and bought up all kinds of wine and booze and brought it back to the ship to celebrate.

Harold Wellington took this photo on a Liberty ship.

Harold continued, "I went through the whole war in the Merchant Marine and got out in 1946 as a licensed fireman, water tender, and oiler."

Surprise: The Draft Board Called

"When I left to go into the service I told my dad, 'I ain't never coming back to the farm. I've played nursemaid to cows as long as I'm gonna.' So when I came back to Vermont in '46, I went and got a job in an auto body shop.

"In 1948 the Army called me and said, 'You've never been in the service.' They went and drafted me into the Army. I'd been through the whole war in a service that had the highest fatality rate except for the Marine Corps, because of the sinkings of our ships by German air strikes and submarines. Hell, we were getting blown all to pieces. And they say, 'You've never been in the service.' So I spent a little over a year in the Army, which I hated. After a little over a year, they said, 'We're not going to discharge you. We're going to release you for the convenience of the government. But you're going to spend six years in the Reserve.'"

Harold (on the left) relaxing with a buddy on a Liberty Ship around 1943

147

In the Navy

"I came home from the Army and seven months later, I got a letter from the draft board and was called back in. But there was no way I was going back in the Army because I hated it. So I went back to the Navy office and this time they said, 'You join the Navy and we'll get you released from the Army.' So that's what I did.

"I spent all of the Korean War in the Navy, but not in Korea. I was stationed on the east coast of the U.S. and traveled to Copenhagen, Denmark and Lisbon, Portugal. I was Second Class Boilerman and discharged in 1954.

"Then I came back home and went back to work in the auto body shop. I did that for most of the rest of my life. In 1988, the government declared the Merchant Marine a part of the Coast Guard. I received an official discharge from the Coast Guard and the benefits that went with it.

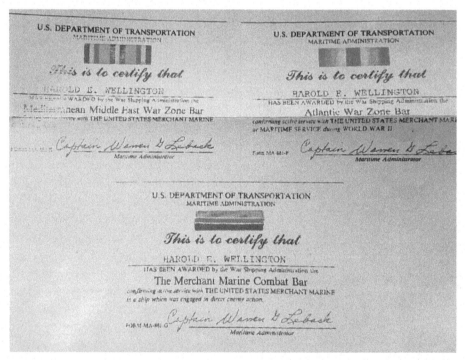

Certificates accompanying Harold Wellington's bars for Merchant Marine Service
- Mediterranean Middle East War Zone Bar
- Atlantic War Zone Bar
- Merchant Marine Combat Bar

"After I retired, I was in South Carolina with a national camping club. That's where I met my wife Martha—camping. I was 66 years old and got married for the first time. She had two children who were still living. I was lucky to have these two stepchildren, who took me in and have been great to me. Martha and I lived in Brevard since 1989, which was her home. She passed away in 2015."

Harold and Martha Wellington on Harold's 90th birthday at a Navy reunion in 2014. Harold still fit into his Navy uniform!

In retirement, Harold has made hundreds of wooden toys which he donates to children through a home for battered women, the sheriff's department, and the motorcycle veterans' toy drive. He also keeps small handmade toys in his pocket when he goes to restaurants and gives the toys to children he sees there.

In this 2016 picture Harold is holding a hand-crafted white squirrel, Brevard's mascot. He gave a similar one to a favorite waitress at his frequent breakfast restaurant, Creekside. On the bookcase above are Harold's prototypes for many of the toys he designs and makes.

149

Vernon Rogers Edney, U.S. Army

PFC Vernon Edney, U. S. Army

Vernon Edney served in the U.S. Army from July 27, 1942 to September 10, 1945. He served with Company F, 157ᵗʰ Infantry in Sicily, Battle of the Bulge, Naples-Foggia Campaign, Rome-Arno Campaign, Southern France, Rhineland, and Central Europe.

I'd Rather Be in the Army than Picking Peas

Vernon Edney told these stories to his wife. "In the summer of 1942, me and Flournoy Edney were picking peas in a field in Edneyville, North Carolina. I hated picking peas! I told Flournoy, 'I'd rather be in the Army than picking peas.' Well, it wasn't long till I was in the Army. I was drafted in August of 1942 and sent to Fort Jackson, South Carolina, joining the 45ᵗʰ Thunderbird, a veteran division from Oklahoma originally made up of American Indians.

"From there I was sent to Camp Roberts, California, for 16 weeks of basic training. We went by train through Texas. I woke up three mornings and asked where we were. 'We're still in Texas!' they told me. At Camp Roberts the parade field was so big you could have marched every service man in the country on it at the same time!

"Then we went to Pine Camp, New York, where it was 42 degrees below zero one Sunday. Everything was covered in snow. I never saw the earth the whole time I was there. It was my first year ever away from home at Christmas and I wasn't dreaming of a white Christmas—I was in one! That was the year Bing Crosby came out with the song.

"From there we went to Camp Pickett, Virginia, where we trained with the Navy in Chesapeake Bay for amphibious landing. We didn't know at the time, but it was for the invasion of Sicily. But I knew we were going overseas by our training and the waterproofing of all the equipment."

To Africa and Italy

"On June 3, 1943, we were on the U.S.S. Thomas Jefferson transport ship in Hampton Roads, Virginia. Along with two other transport ships, we were ready to ship out. We picked up more ships all up and down the east coast. At the time, it was the biggest convoy ever to sail—500 ships. The enemy planes and subs did not attack us.

"After an uneventful landing in Oran, Africa, on June 23, 1943, we sailed to Sicily, Italy, landing on July 10. They said it was the roughest weather they'd had in 100 years, but we were coordinated with other American ships and English ships, so we couldn't call it off. We landed safely on a smooth beach, but some landed on rocks and broke up the Higgins boats. They found men dead on the rocks four days later. There was heavy barrage by our naval guns so the other three battalions would get in under cover of fire.

"On land, we walked through a vineyard first. I was nauseous from the rough sailing. I ate some grapes and that helped some. In the early morning hours of July 11, with the help of another battalion, we captured the Comiso Airport, where German forces had been stationed. [This operation was under the command of (then) Lieutenant General Omar Bradley.] We took over the airport and used it to support Allied airborne and assault glider operations. We took over planes, gasoline, and, as a joke, a nickel-plated bicycle. Our chaplain, Leland L. Loy, rode that bike up and down the hills of Sicily and carried stuff to the men who were tired.

"We made a long march to Cerda to establish roadblocks at a rail junction. In the early morning hours of July 23, within a mile of Cerda, the 2nd Battalion was ambushed on an open road. We took what cover we could in shallow places in the ground and sweated out 50 minutes of hell. Then the Germans blew up a bridge, throwing chunks of cement into the

prostrate men. The 158th Field Artillery dropped a barrage and pinned them down, and allowed our battalion to withdraw and try to outflank the Germans, but they had made their famous withdrawal. [When Patton's American soldiers moved into Messina, Sicily, expecting to fight one final battle, Patton was surprised to learn that the enemy forces had disappeared. The battle for Sicily was complete.]

"We rested and went on to San Stefano—from Caltavutro. Between these two towns were a series of ridges. Then all hell broke loose. Mortar fire and machine guns pounded as we went forward through lemon and olive groves. First and 3rd Battalions captured the high ground northwest of the town after fighting all day. In the morning the 2nd Battalion captured Germans who were still asleep. There was hard, bitter fighting all day. A visiting general said, 'What a bloody ridge this was!' giving the battle its name. I knew one man who got hold of some bad wine and got drunk and was lying face-down throwing up in the sand and he would have choked if I hadn't rolled him over out of it."

Taking Sicily

"We took Sicily [Operation Husky], but at a great cost. But to the 157th Infantry troops, Sicily was a first step toward home the hard way. In Sicily we saw Bob Hope and Frances Langford [American singer and movie star], who put on a good show. She was the first woman we'd seen since we left Virginia. I sat on a hill looking right down at the stage. It was like sitting on the 50-yard line. They [Hope and Langford] went to Palermo to stay the night and we saw the German planes bomb the harbor there, trying to sink ships.

"Our men were shooting ack-ack [anti-aircraft artillery] at them. That was a big show too. There's never been any 4th of July show to equal it.

"General Patton spoke to us and told us if we were dumb enough to let the Germans slip up behind us and hit us over the head with a sock full of s---, that's what we deserved. He congratulated us too. But we sure enjoyed Bob Hope and Frances Langford. We were lucky to get to see that. Talked about it for five days.

"We had been relieved by the 3rd Division of the American 7th Army. That was the end of our first 21 days of combat in WWII, and the end of the costly Bloody Ridge engagement. We rested, washed in streams, and raided watermelon patches."

Salerno and Rome

"We invaded Salerno from Sicily on LCI [Landing Craft Infantry] on September 8, 1943, on the way to mainland Italy. Italy surrendered and it was announced over loudspeakers. The troops went wild and dreamed of home. But Col. Preston Murphy announced, 'Remember, Germany hasn't surrendered.' We pushed on to Rome September 15. Our tanks could have gone on into Rome if they'd had some artillery protection. We were camped outside of Rome. On Saturday our CO [commanding officer] said if any of us were Catholic we could go into Rome to one of the cathedrals for Mass. An old boy from Kentucky yelled back and said, 'What about all of us hard shelled Baptists?' Well, on Sunday morning we were all Catholics and went into Rome.

Vernon Edney in Italy or France

154

"As we moved east and north across Italy, we had strafing by enemy aircraft. I jumped behind a rock wall and shot at the airplanes with my rifle. We marched 15 miles to Charamonte and took garrisons at Elmo and Montercosa. Then at Licodia the Germans struck back. In eight days we walked 130 miles facing hot sun and enemy guns. We ate grapes, peaches, watermelons, and figs. But this led to widespread diseases—one of our men died. His folks were told he was killed in action. He was!

"I had malaria in Italy and was in a tent hospital. Me and the other guys would open our IV tubes to make it go faster and the nurses would fuss at us. When the alarms sounded the nurses would grab the helmets and head for the air raid shelter.

"There were trenches all over Italy. We saw Mussolini's farm and dead cows all over the trenches lying on their backs with feet up in the air, killed by shrapnel. Mussolini must have dug the trenches to hold us off.

"I didn't think too much of Rome. I just remember being drunk and crawling all around the coliseum It seemed like a bunch of rubble. Rome didn't seem any different at that time than any other town we had been in."

Apennines Mountains, Italy

"On the 7th of November, 1943, the 157th went up the Appenines—the mountains we called them. We bivouacked on the side of a steep mountain. First Battalion moved its way high into the Apennines on November 9, to help some American paratroopers who were stranded there. The men ran into small arms fire from Germans dug in and impossible to locate. Enemy mortars were used with success. But when the German planes came over, the planes and the men on the line both came under fire by anti-aircraft guns from far below. No more towns, just hill numbers. Then the winter line was under siege.

"We put cigarettes in our foxholes to soak up the water. It was so cold after a rain our machine guns were frozen and we couldn't have fired them if we needed to. We wore our wool pants and jackets summer and winter—same underwear for months. The ground was frozen. We couldn't dig a foxhole so we piled up rocks around us like a room and put our pup tents over them to keep warm. How we ever survived with only our uniform (no long-johns) and one blanket is a miracle.

"They brought up our supplies on mules because they could climb the steep rocks; horses could not, and the helicopter was not in the army yet. Sometimes the mules gave out and supplies had to be brought in by weary soldiers. Our K-rations came in a box a little bigger than a cracker-jack box. It had three meals in it, a pack of instant coffee and a little can of ham and eggs we could heat by burning the K-ration box. We could hold our canteen of water over the burning K-ration box to heat the water to make coffee. The only eating utensil we had was a spoon we carried in our right rear pocket.

"Men had trench foot, couldn't walk. It was Valley Forge, 1943. Men and mules lived together in misery.

"Once we were looking for a German bunker and found ourselves surrounded by Germans. They started to march us back behind their lines as POWs. Germans or Americans started shelling in our direction so we all hit the ground. I got in a ditch and started crawling backward. I got out of sight and back to our company. It was a close call. If they had seen me trying to escape, they probably would have shot me. I saw my buddies after the war at a reunion and one of them asked me where I was when they got captured. I told them, 'I wasn't as stupid as you Yankee guys—I got away.'

"We had been in Rome for R&R. From there we went up the coast and back on a ship to make our landing at Anzio, January 22, 1944. That's where some shrapnel from a tank hit me on the back of my helmet, made a hole in it, and imbedded shrapnel or metal in the back of my head. I have a scar about the size of a 50-cent piece. I left my helmet there, I guess. Sure wish I had it now. Some metal was imbedded in my left wrist too. Later I broke my wrist when I walked off the end of a railroad track where the tracks had been blown up. Once I came out of my dugout and a shell came and landed almost between my legs. It happened to be a dud or I would have been gone."

Vernon Edney in Italy or France

Southern France

"We fought our way into southern France, September 4, 1944, and were heading for Germany. We found a farmer having trouble delivering a calf from its mother cow. We stopped and helped him. The 'Stars and Stripes' printed the story under the title: *Surrounded by New Yorkers who had never seen such things before, Pfc. Vernon Edney, Hendersonville, N.C., was midwife to a cow during a barrage the other night. Mother and daughter are doing well.*

"Once in Southern France a farm family let us sleep downstairs under their living quarters with the livestock. That made it warm. A baby was crying upstairs and one of the guys said, 'Dammit, they cry like our babies—why can't they talk like us?'

The French were glad to see us and treated us well. We were their liberators. I traded an old army folding cot with canvas on it to a Frenchman for a bottle of Champagne. Next time I got two bottles for a cot!

"While in France in the Argonne Forest we found trenches from World War I where the armies fought. I found an old canteen there.

"We crossed the Rhine River. After we took Berlin on March 29, 1945, I joined the 123rd Ordinance Ammo Company on April 28, 1945 while we were in Germany. I drove a Jeep to Switzerland every other day, carrying papers. I had the fastest jeep in Germany.

"I got word my father was very ill and was asking to see me, but I couldn't get leave. He died and I never got to see him.

"The war was over May 8, 1945. I liked the work at the Ammo Company and wouldn't have cared if the war was never over. I went to Austria, Belgium, and then back to New York on September 6, 1945. We didn't know we were saved from attacking Japan by the atomic bomb till later."

Pfc. Vernon Edney and his medals

Vernon had four amphibious landings and six campaigns. He was awarded six Bronze Service Stars, the Distinguished Unit Badge and the Purple Heart.

At right, Pfc. Vernon Edney's medals and insignia: six Bronze Service Stars, the Rifleman's Badge, the Distinguished Unit Badge, and the Purple Heart.

Vernon said, "I went through hell and back to Hendersonville."

After the War

When Vernon and Faye Lance began dating (both pictured below) in 1950, people said he looked like the actor and dancer Gene Kelley. Faye said he always answered, "Yes, but he can't dance like I can!"

Vernon and Faye, who was from Mills River, N.C., married in 1952. After his discharge from the Army, he worked in a filling station and a smoke shop. He and Faye built and operated a skating rink for 18 years. He became a carpenter, building houses and putting on roofs and porches. He bought a cabin in Mills River where he enjoyed staying when deer hunting.

Vernon Edney passed away April 4, 2006. He had told these stories to his wife, Faye, over a period of nine years. Faye has lovingly written and organized Vernon's experiences into an important history, told in a personal way. She generously shares copies with everyone who is interested. She especially likes to give copies to young people. This story is excerpted from Faye's beautiful tribute to her husband.

Faye Edney in 2016

"WE SHALL COME HOME VICTORIOUS."

ARMY

Elizabeth Ellen Churchill Frodsham Tilston
British Army Auxiliary Transport Service, Women's Division

Elizabeth Tilston, Ambulance Driver, British Army Auxiliary Transport Service

*Elizabeth Tilston worked as a driver in the British Army's Auxiliary Transport Service
from 1942 to 1947.*

I Want to Join the Army

Elizabeth Ellen Churchill Tilston tells her story of joining the service. "All my friends had gone into the Army. I thought I wanted to do that. I had a very good family. I was never smacked, but if I misbehaved, I was told what I had done and why I shouldn't do it. And then I had to go to my room. That was the only punishment.

"I'm grateful for that, because that made me tell the truth and do the things I should've done in the first place.

"Then the war started when I was young, living at home. Firebombs would be coming down and the sirens would go off. My father had built an air raid shelter and our whole family—six children—would go down there, underground, and stay until the signal came that it was safe to come out. It happened every day. We had food and water and air mattresses. When we were at school, we had shelters and we did the same thing. I don't ever remember being terribly afraid. I just did what I was supposed to do.

"I wanted to join the Army. We lived in a place called Maghull, which is outside of Southport in the North of England. I went to join and they said, 'You have to be seventeen.' And I said, 'Well, I'm only three months off seventeen.' So they said, 'O.K., we'll take all your particulars down now, but you can't start until you turn seventeen.' I decided I'd better go home and tell my parents what I'd done. They were furious with me. They said, 'Well, you're not going because you're underage, and we can cancel that very easily.' I said, 'Oh, please don't do that. Please give me a chance.' So they said, 'O.K., we'll let you go for one month. We'll visit you for lunch and if we find that you can't cope, you're out.'

"And that's what they did. They came to lunch. My training was in the south of England, a long way from Maghull. But by this time, I had made a friend. We had fun together, real fun. I asked my friend to come with me to lunch with my parents and she did. During lunch, my parents saw that my friend and I were having fun together. At the end of the luncheon, they said, 'O.K. You win.' So I stayed in."

I Want to Be a Driver

"I knew I wanted to be a driver to help people. My father had taught me to drive. Not many people had cars, but my father had a car. I loved to drive and I was very good at it. I became a driver. At the end of the war I drove soldiers to the hospitals or transferred them from one hospital to another [within Great Britain]. I never felt in danger myself. The roads were easy to see. We had maps or they would tell us how to go. Sometimes I drove in the tunnel under the river from Liverpool to Birkenhead. I always thought that was really fantastic.

"I drove an ambulance until one day, when my boss said, 'You're going to drive General Charles De Gaulle.' [De Gaulle was then leader of the Free French Forces against the Axis and the French government in exile in England.] Why they picked me, I don't know, because I was just driving an ambulance, but I was a good driver. They gave me an Army Jaguar. I picked him up in Liverpool and drove him around for a week. He was a big man. He would sit in the back seat. He didn't talk much, but if I asked him a question, he would answer nicely. He spoke English. He traveled alone. I would take him to his appointments and then go into the building and wait for him. At the end of the week, he shook hands with me, said 'Thank you,' and that was it. Then I went back to my ambulance."

Meeting the Future Queen

"In the Army we attended many classes, of course. I met Princess Elizabeth in a class before she became Queen," Elizabeth remembered. "She was in the Army too, you know. She was very nice. Six of us were in a course together for a week. I met her several times after that and we stayed in touch."

The War Ends and the Soldiers Come Home

"Finally, the war was over. All my girl friends in the Army wanted to go to a pub to celebrate. They wanted me to come, but I didn't want to go. I was very prim and proper. I didn't have boyfriends, I had girl friends. The boys joined in with us sometimes, but I wasn't one of those flirty things. I told my friends, 'I don't drink.' They said, 'You're going!' So I said, 'Well, O.K.'

"In the pub, I was buying a ginger ale at the bar for myself and my girl friend who never had any money, and this pilot officer came up to me and started chatting. I thought, 'Some nerve. I don't even know him and he comes up and starts talking.' He said, 'Come and sit with us [a table with his buddies].' I said, 'No. I'm with my friends.' So I went back to my friends. They had heard there was going to be a dance and they wanted to go, so I went.

R.A.F. Pilot Edwin Tilston

"At the dance, this man comes up to me again and said, 'May I have this dance?' I said, 'No!' The girls said, 'Oh, go on and dance.' I said, 'No, I'm not,' and I sat down. Then he came up again, got hold of my hand, and pulled me up to my feet. He said, 'We're going to dance.' We danced every dance for the rest of the night. And then he met me every night where I was billeted.

"He came every night at six o'clock because that's when I finished my work. And he would take me for a walk, very good, very proper. Never tried to kiss me or anything like that.

"His name was Edwin. After two weeks, he got hold of my hand, he put a ring on my finger, and he said, 'Now we are engaged.' He hadn't even kissed me or put his arm around me or anything. Then I had to go home and tell my parents. I got home about eleven o'clock in the evening, and I knocked on my parents' bedroom door. You never, ever went into your parents' bedroom. But I knocked, and my mother said, 'Who is it?' I said, 'It's me, Mummy. I need to just chat with you for a moment.' She said, 'Come in.' I went in. She said, 'Are you all right?' 'I'm fine, Mummy.' 'Well, what's wrong?' 'I'm engaged.'

"My father shot up out of bed. He said, 'Did I hear you say you're engaged?!' I said, 'Yes, Daddy, you heard right. But don't worry; he's coming tomorrow morning to meet you.' He came, they loved him on sight and he loved them. And that was the beginning. I had a wonderful life after that.

"After the war was over, my job as ambulance driver was especially sad. The ships would come into the Liverpool docks bringing home prisoners of war the Germans had held for God knows how long. The soldiers were in very bad shape. When the ships came in, I would work day and night without sleep. Other people carried the men on a stretcher; I only had to drive. Edwin and I were engaged then. When he was on leave, he would follow me on his motorcycle wherever I went driving the ambulance, to make sure nothing happened to me and I got there all right.

"Then I got out of the Army. My husband Edwin, then a pilot, got out of the Air Force and joined the Fleet Air Arm so that he could continue flying after the war. Later he became an agent for Lloyds of London. We got married six months after he put that ring on my finger and said, 'Now we're engaged.'"

Edwin and Elizabeth on their wedding day

Traveling the World

"Ed's company sent him to their Portugal office to solve a problem. At that time I was pregnant with my daughter, so I stayed with my parents in England to have my baby. But

later I went with him to places all over the world with his business. Then we had a son. We put both our children in boarding schools in England so they wouldn't be moving around so often, and I went with Ed.

At left: Elizabeth Tilston, a few years after World War II ended

"Wherever we traveled, Ed was assigned to be Honorary British Consul if there was no Consul in that country. He met with the leaders of the countries. For instance, we became good friends with the president of Peru and his wife. We were invited to all the parties by heads of government wherever we went. Every country we went to was fantastic. It was a wonderful life. I don't know anyone who has had a life like mine.

Elizabeth dancing at a party

"Ed eventually founded his own steamship company. We went back to England, bought a lovely house, and were expecting to live there for the rest of our lives. But then business called, and we moved to New York and later New Orleans. I loved it all. When it was time to retire, we came to Brevard. We had visited it many times and knew how beautiful it was. Unfortunately, Ed passed away several years ago.

"I've lived in Connestee Falls [in Brevard, North Carolina] since 1999. By the way, I'm 91 and still driving. I've only had one accident in my life, and it wasn't my fault. My father taught me well."

Elizabeth Tilston in 2016

Sanford Groendyke, U.S. Army Air Corps

Sanford Groendyke, U.S. Army Air Corps Pilot

Sandy Groendyke joined the U.S. Army Air Corps in 1943 and served as a B-17 Bomber pilot in Europe. After his plane was hit and was forced to land, he was captured and held in a German prison camp for nine months. Thise photo was taken after Sandy's wife, Mary Helen, had pinned his wings on.

Airplanes

Sandy tells his story: "I finished high school in 1939 in High Bridge, New Jersey. I moved to Newark, which was nearby, and I roomed with a man who was the world champion of free-flight model airplanes. They had a little gasoline engine. We would build model planes and go to meets on the weekends. That was our basic interest. We decided to go to Casey Jones School of Aeronautics at night. The school was right in Newark. He was taking engineering and I was taking the ground school. And the war broke out.

"The government got us all together and said 'We want you to quit your jobs and go to school full-time. We'll pay the tuition and we'll pay you a per diem to live on. All you have to agree to is to work for the government when you graduate.' Sounded like a good deal! We'd get our education and a job would be waiting for us when we graduated in the field that we enjoyed. The food trucks were outside the school and that's where we would gather. A guy says, 'What are we doing here in this school? We all want to fly airplanes. Why don't we go down to the post office where all the military branches have offices? We'll see about taking the exam for cadet.' 'Yeah, yeah, we said.' So a bunch of us went down and took the initial test. It was easy. We kept going back and taking more tests.

"I had no problems whatsoever, so I graduated and they sent me up to a new air field that was being built for West Point cadets. I was in the ground crew and was an electrician at that point. The plane I worked on had a lot of problems with the electrical system. So I aced it all and passed all the tests. The only problem was that the flying schools were all full and it would be about six months before there would be an opening. They said, 'We don't want to lose you to the draft. So we'll put you in the reserve, subject to call. You'll be an officer when you graduate.'"

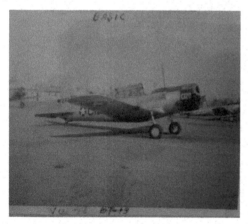 

In the Army Air Corps: Flight School

"That was 1943. I took more tests and qualified for a flying position. They always ask you which one you want: pilot, navigator, or bombardier. I always said pilot first. We went to flight training in Helena, Arkansas. It was a civilian school that, because of the war, was used for military training. That's where I really learned to fly an airplane.

"The planes didn't have radios. We were taught the basics of flying and you were able to pass the solo test with no instructor there to help you. So I soloed the plane using pilotage—using things you can see on the ground—highways, rivers, what you can see. You're navigating the airplane mechanically. You fly to an airport, land, get somebody to sign your logbook, and fly back. So that was the solo cross-country. The training ended there and the next flight school was in Arkansas.

"The next plane I flew had a radio and a light gun that had a hood on it so that the light from the control tower went out. You look at the tower and they're shooting this at you. A red light meant you couldn't land. A green light meant you could land. You had to watch this. A red light could mean that another plane was in the space. We had some elementary aerobatics—loops, spins. I always liked spins. When you do a spin, you throttle back and get more angle. Now you're in a stall position. If you kick the rudder for a right turn you would stall and your nose would go straight down toward the ground. When you decide you've had enough of that—getting too close to the ground, you stop the turn and up the stick to break the stall. We had learned these stalls and spins with an instructor initially, and practiced once when I earned my wings."

Meeting Mary Helen at Church

"My friend Hank said, 'Let's go into the town—Jonesboro—and see what it looks like.' I said OK. Hank was married, but you couldn't have your wife with you at that base. I didn't have a girlfriend at the time. So we went to town, went to a movie, danced a little, and got a hotel room. Hank said, 'What do you want to do tomorrow?' I said 'Go to church.' I was Dutch Reform from New York City—New Amsterdam—but I knew they wouldn't have that church there. Hank was Baptist. I said, 'I've never been, but that's OK.' Hank said, 'Well how about Sunday School?' I said, 'I'm a Yankee. We don't go to Sunday School after the 8th grade.' Hank said, 'We Baptists go to Sunday School to our grave.'

"I said, 'Well you go to Sunday School and I'll meet you after and go to the service.' I met him there, and the choir came in. There were four girls in the choir. I'd say in their early twenties. I looked at one in particular. I said 'Boy, I'd love to meet her. But there's not a chance in hell. She'll go home and have dinner with her family and if we're lucky, we might get somebody to invite us to dinner—we'll get a decent meal—we were in our uniforms. So I put the idea of meeting her out of my mind, but then she sang a solo. The service was over. We were out in front of the church talking to the locals—where are you from and so forth—trying to get somebody to invite us to eat.

"This girl comes up and tugs on Hank's arm and invites him to the Baptist Student Union class and says, 'It would be OK if your friend would like to come, too.' I said, 'Yeah, let's do it!' So we went down and it turned out that she had her eye on me and I had my eye on her. Honest to goodness, it was just sheer love. Her name was Mary Helen. I got her phone number before I left and I called her every Wednesday. She liked me or my looks, so I hitchhiked in my uniform to see her every weekend. We called that the Arkansas taxicab. Everybody had a pickup truck—farmers, you know.

"I got to the next school. I was graduating from cadets. Mary Helen had an aunt and uncle right on the edge of the base where I was assigned. It came to the time that Mary Helen and I were a couple. At graduation I gave her a ring. She had never met my family. We had two weeks of vacation, so we hopped a train to New Jersey and spent a few days with my parents.

"My next base was in Ohio. It was Christmas time. We were engaged. I had my car now, so I drove back to Arkansas. Mary Helen had graduated from the state college where she could live at home and for a nickel she could ride the bus to college. I got jaundice and went to the hospital there. They kept me for a while and then decided they couldn't do any more for me, so they let me out. I went back to the commander. He said, 'I don't know what to do with you. Your class has left while you were in the hospital. The next thing to do is to go to Florida where they make up the crews. But Florida's not ready for you yet, so I can't send you there. I'll tell you what I can do. I'll cut orders for you and you can report in four weeks.'"

A Wedding

"I went to the phone and called Mary Helen. 'Two weeks' vacation—what do you think about getting married?' She said, 'I think that's a wonderful idea!' I said, 'I'll be there tomorrow.' This didn't quite jive with her mother, but she prayed about it and the next day she said OK. It was June. Everybody had flowers in their garden, she had bridesmaids from her choral group who had all gone to high school together. So we had a church wedding and her mother gave her away. Her father had been deceased when she was six, so it was just her mother. Her mother had plans to go to California where Mary Helen's brother lived and get her master's degree."

Below, Sandy and Mary Helen Groendyke

"So we were newlyweds. We went to Florida and got there ahead of time. We got a motel. When we got up the next morning and came down to breakfast, people asked us, 'Have you heard?' 'Heard what?' 'It's D-Day! The invasion has started!' So here we were. Somebody asked me later, 'Where were you on D-Day?' I said. 'I was on my honeymoon.'

"In Florida, I was putting my crew together. I got a co-pilot. He had just graduated the week before. He had never been in a B-17, so I had to teach him to fly it. Then we went to Mississippi for six weeks training with the crew for combat.

"Next, we went to Savannah, Georgia, and stayed in a tourist court. We had a hot plate and a refrigerator. Two other guys in my crew came in with no place to stay, so they stayed with us. One slept in the bathtub, one on the floor."

Mary Helen (third from left), Sandy (fourth from left) and Sandy's crew and another wife

Heading to War in Europe

"We picked up a brand-new B-17 bomber (photo below). We checked it out to make sure everything was working. We had the official orders to go to Labrador. We had to avoid a hurricane to get there. Our next destination was Reykjavik, Iceland. We had to wait for the weather to break. Finally, we flew to Wales. We turned in our airplane and they put us on a train to a base sixty miles northeast. We were there till October 2, then we flew over Germany. I had a seasoned crew. I took the co-pilot position to experience combat. The pilot came from Trenton, New Jersey, which was only 30 miles from where I was from. So we became good friends, of course.

Sandy's crew

"The pilot would be in control of the plane for 15 minutes and then the co-pilot would take control for 15 minutes. This was to minimize fatigue and stress.

"The Germans were pretty good at shooting at us. The first day, we took some flak. The crew said, 'Oh, that's usual.' The second day, October 3, we took a direct hit which killed the bombardier. He lived about 15 minutes. The propellers on each side of him were knocked out, so we "feathered" the props. This enabled more air to come through because there was less resistance. So we kept the two other engines running part-time but never at the same time. It was a hard thing to control, but it allowed us to get a little farther away. We were at about 24,000 feet when we were hit."

Our Target Was Nuremburg

"Our target was Nuremburg. We knew what the winds were, we had had a weather forecast during our briefing. There was a cloud cover at 6500 base and the tops were at 10,000. We had been briefed about this. The navigator was trying to help the bombardier before he died, so he didn't know where we were. But we knew where we were.

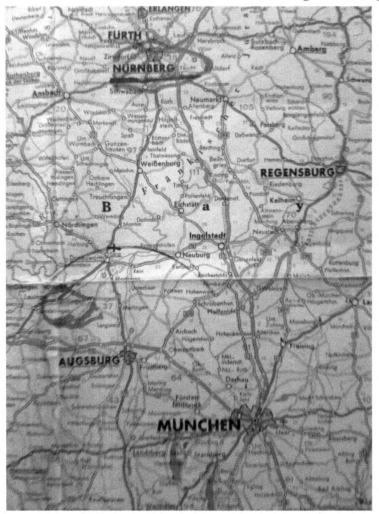

The arrow on this map shows the field where Sandy and his crew made the emergency landing.

"We knew we couldn't get back to England. We knew the nearest friendly was Switzerland. We kept going down and down and down. We got down to about 12,000 feet and called our crew in the back and said, 'Anybody wants to bail out, do it now.' They called us back and said, 'We're with you. We're going down with you.' We had opened the bomb bay doors where the crew could bail out if they chose to. We didn't know this until several days later, but they had one guy who picked up a parachute. They asked him, 'Where are you going?' He said, 'Getting the hell out." They said, 'No, you're not." They took the parachute and threw it out the bomb bay door. So they made him stay with us. We didn't wear our parachutes. We wore harnesses with two rings, then we could clip the parachute to those rings when we needed to."

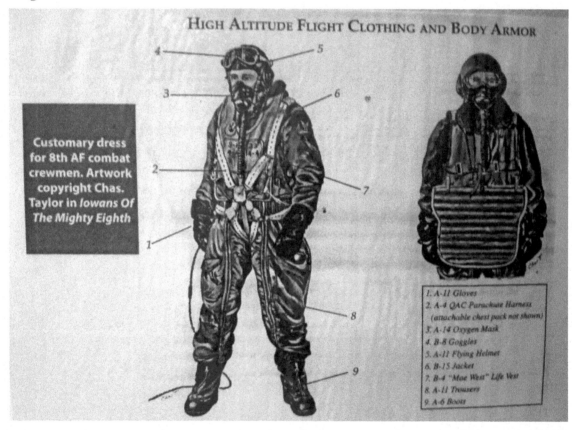

HIGH ALTITUDE FLIGHT CLOTHING AND BODY ARMOR

Customary dress for 8th AF combat crewmen. Artwork copyright Chas. Taylor in *Iowans Of The Mighty Eighth*

1. A-11 Gloves
2. A-4 QAC Parachute Harness (attachable chest pack not shown)
3. A-14 Oxygen Mask
4. B-8 Goggles
5. A-11 Flying Helmet
6. B-15 Jacket
7. B-4 "Mae West" Life Vest
8. A-11 Trousers
9. A-6 Boots

Emergency Landing

"We were northwest of Munich. We went down through the cloud cover and saw the most beautiful farmland. Beautiful. So we started looking for a field to land in. I asked my co-pilot to pick a place to land. I had picked the same spot. So we landed. This little town was maybe 30 houses or so. There were trees on one end. Where we landed was slightly uphill. The wind was just right. We had been trained to check the wind by finding smoke or clothes on a clothesline—to see which way they were blowing.

We had to go through a fence when we landed. They fence blew apart like toothpicks. It broke the plexiglass cover where the bombardier and navigator were (see nose of plane in diagram below). The bombardier, who was dead now, fell out.

Below, a map showing the field where Sandy landed the plant. X marks the spot where the bombardier, who had died, fell out when the plexiglass broke.

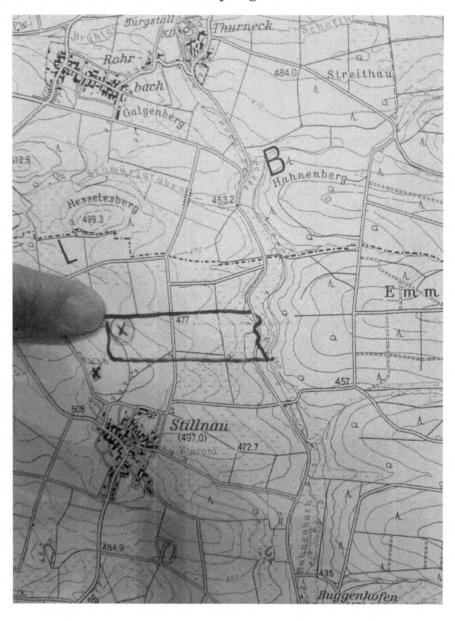

"Nobody even got a scratch during that landing. We followed procedures and you only make one landing. It's a good one or a bad one. But you practice a lot, you know. Everything worked out well because we had our lives.

"The people were harvesting grain. Everything was done by hand, with a scythe, no machinery. They were starving, the German people. While we were circling the field to land, the people saw us. They went off to the sides to wait for us to land. We got out of the plane calmly. We didn't have any guns. We had thrown everything we could off the plane to make it lighter. We had bombs but no guns. The people had guns, so there was nothing we could do. They had guns to protect their food. People were starving. So they took us to the village and put us in a building.

"We went back 30 years later and got this picture (right). We didn't know it at the time, but this was a 14th century building that had been used by farmers to store their property. There was no law enforcement back then, so they would put their food in this building to secure it."

Captured and Sent to a German Prison Camp

"We were kept in this building until nightfall, when the Luftwaffe came in their 'six-by' truck—a truck with a canvas top. There were nine of us prisoners, everyone except our bombardier who had been killed. They took us to the Luftwaffe base, probably 150-200 miles from where we had landed. They treated us like gentlemen. We offered no resistance. We were fliers, not fighters.

"They took us to their base and gave us a nice meal and bunked us down. It was on the floor but had some straw ticks we could sleep on. They gave us breakfast. Guards took us to an interrogation place on the Mainz River. It took us three days to get there. They took us to a stone building. No heat, of course. Individual cells, we were in solitary. They'd give us soup for lunch. One meal a day, we got. It was lousy. They would interrogate us one by one. They tried to get information. All we would give them was our name, rank, and serial number. That's all that was required. They tried to lure you in. Those days, everybody smoked. They had cigarettes they would offer. Where they got them, I don't know, but they had them.

"They kept calling one of our guys back. They knew a lot of personal information about him and he couldn't figure out why. They knew he lived in Princeton, New Jersey. Finally, he asked them, 'Where did you get all this information?' The interrogator said, 'Did you and Mary ever get married?' He said, 'How do you know all this stuff?' The interrogator said, 'It was easy. You lived on such-and-such street. I lived on such-and-such street. It was two blocks over. You were my paper boy.' Can you imagine that?' Well, when the war first started, a lot of people who had come to the States from Germany went back. Their allegiance was really to their homeland. That's what this guy had done, and why he spoke English. It's hard to believe, but it's true.

"We were under interrogation for about six days or so. One morning, they told us to get our stuff and fall out. We didn't have any stuff, but we got down there and got on a train. We were all happy to see each other after being in solitary. That's when we found out that the one guy had wanted to jump out with a parachute and they threw his chute out. They put us on a train and sent us way up to their prison camp on the Baltic."

Lt. Goenbyke Is Missing

Husband Of Former Mary Helen Davis Missing In Air Action

Lieutenant Stanley Groenbyke was reported missing in action over Germany on Oct. 3 according to information received by friends in this city from his wife, the former Mary Helen Davis.

Lieutenant Groenbyke was on his second mission. He was formerly stationed at Walnut Ridge and Blytheville. His home was in New Jersey.

Mrs. Groenbyke makes her home with her mother in California. She was a popular student at Arkansas State College for several years.

Above, the newspaper article that appeared in New Jersey when Sandy Groendyke was captured (his name is misspelled).

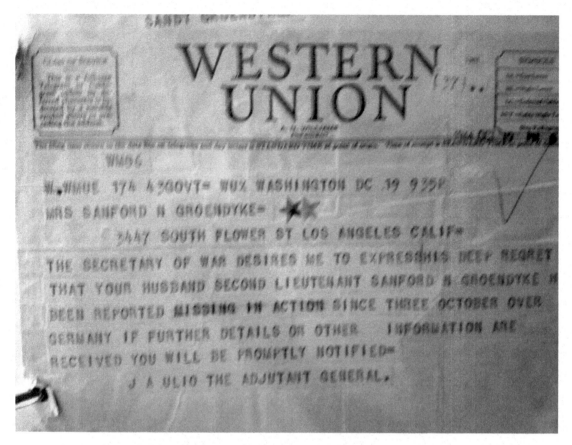

This telegram to Sandy's wife on December 19, 1944 reads: "The Secretary of War desires me to express his deep regret that your husband Second Lieutenant Sanford N. Groendyke has been reported **missing in action** since three October over Germany. If further details or other information are received you will be promptly notified.

J A Ulio the Adjutant General

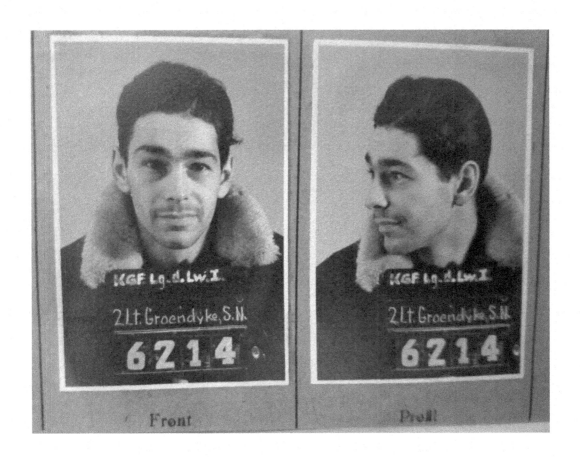

Above, Sanford **"Sandy"** Groendyke's mug shots in the prison camp

Above, map of German prison camps. The camp where Groendyke was held, indicated with white arrow, was across the Baltic Sea from Sweden.

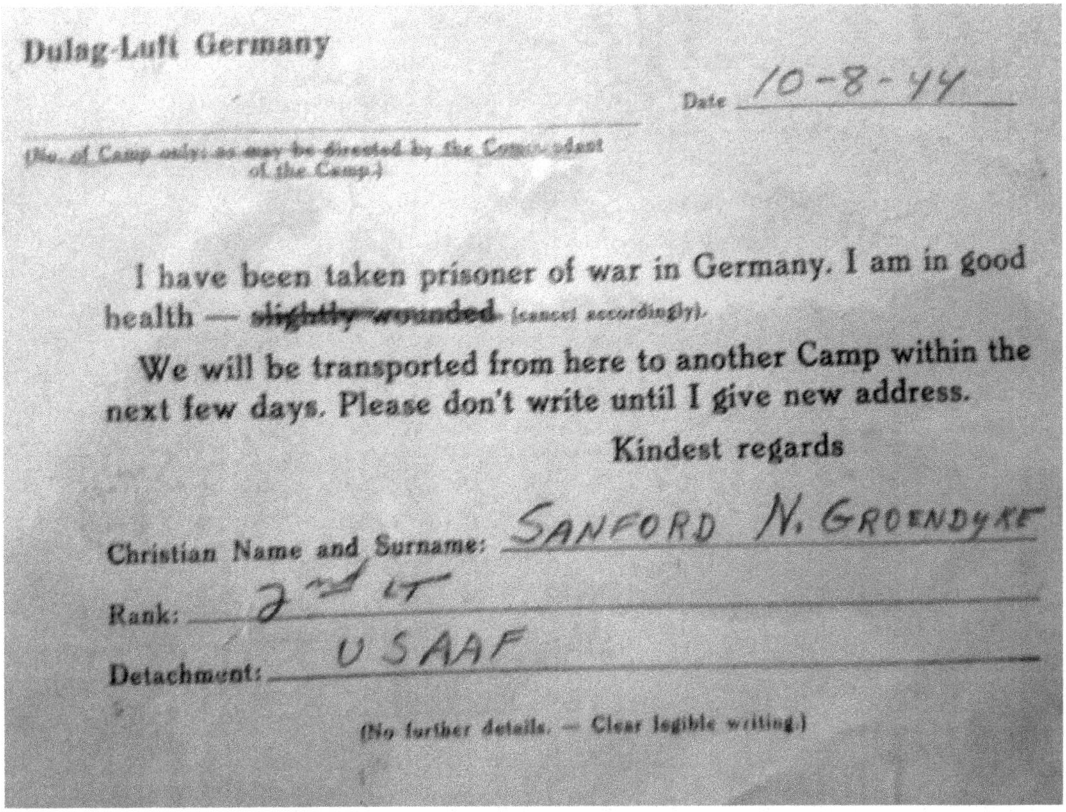

Dulag-Luft Germany

Date 10-8-44

(No. of Camp only: as may be directed by the Commandant of the Camp.)

I have been taken prisoner of war in Germany. I am in good health — slightly wounded (cancel accordingly).

We will be transported from here to another Camp within the next few days. Please don't write until I give new address.

Kindest regards

Christian Name and Surname: SANFORD N. GROENDYKE

Rank: 2nd LT

Detachment: U S A A F

(No further details. — Clear legible writing.)

Second Lieutenant Sandy Groendyke completed this form to notify his family of his imprisonment.

"The camp was actually run by our American officers. They were prisoners. I happened to be in the barracks with the 'wheels'. Their function was like this: if the Germans wanted something done, they had to talk to our senior officers, according to the Geneva Convention. So then the American officers would tell us to do it. We never got orders directly from the Germans. We had English pilots who were non-coms. They cooked the food of the American officers. Those guys were stir-crazy because they had been in there since the beginning of the war.

"We had to go to roll call twice a day. The first one was at 6:00 in the morning. So we would line up and the German would count noses. Then we started playing tricks on the Germans. We had one real short guy. We'd get him to stand at the end of the line where they always started counting. Then after the German moved down the line, the short guy would stoop down and run behind the line and stand at attention at the other end. So the German would end up with one person too many. Then they had to count all over again. We'd play games like that, a bunch of G.I.s

"We'd get the orders of the day. We had an exciting time. We had an ace there who thought that we Americans were getting too cozy with the German guards. So he gave us a loud lecture: 'We are still at war, and these are our enemies!' This guy was real mouthy. He was sincere, though. He was sentenced to die, but the death sentence was never carried out. You know, Hitler protected the POWs because his game was to trade the Allies' POWs for his German officers.

"We were out on a little peninsula. There was a flak gunner out on the beach. There had been a flak school there. They had guns out there shooting at our planes. They were training high school girls to shoot those flak guns. There was a concrete road all the way out to the end where the girls would ride bicycles to get to the guns. When the girls would come, somebody would call out, 'Here they come!' We would all run over to the fence and make catcalls. And the girls would start flipping their skirts up in the back, just teasing us. It's the same the world over.

This drawing shows the view Sandy and his prison-mates had from their prison windows.

"In our camp alone, we had just under 10,000 Air Force officers. Just officers. This was one of two camps like this. It was near the town of Barth. We were right across the open water from Sweden, who was neutral. That's where the Red Cross parcels would come in through Sweden. So they put the Red Cross parcels on a boat and sent them over. They asked for volunteers to go down and unload them. Sure, anything to pass the time. We jumped at the chance. All the things in these parcels were helpful when we were liberated."

How We Survived Nine Months In Prison

"We got Red Cross food, but the German people right outside our gate were starving. The war is starting to end. The Allies had landed and were coming up through France. The Russians were coming like a vise. We were right in the center line. They didn't know where to march us. South of us, POWs in those camps were marched toward the center to keep out of the action. This was March, freezing weather. They gave each one a Red Cross parcel to start with, but that didn't last long. We had none of that. I was so lucky. I didn't get a scratch the whole time. I couldn't even get a Purple Heart—thank God.

"We would save raisins from the Red Cross parcels. We had lots of raisins and we had sugar and oleo. People in America didn't have sugar. They had to have stamps to get sugar. We had lots of it. Every Red Cross parcel had five packs of cigarettes. The guys who didn't smoke used those cigarettes like money to trade for other things.

"We used oleo to make lamps. We called it klim. That was milk spelled backward. We got lots of powdered milk. So called all that extra milk klim. We had small tin cans that had powdered coffee in. When they were empty, we'd use those cans to make our lamps. We melted oleo on the stove in those cans, put a wick in it that we made with a piece of cloth cut from the hem of our pants, and a wire. Then we let it harden. That gave us the wick and the fuel for lamp light. We used those to read after 9:00 pm when they turned the lights off. We called them 'kiege' lights. That word was short for some German word. We didn't want to go to sleep at 9:00 because we hadn't done anything all day and we weren't tired or sleepy.

"We had our own underground newspaper, believe it or not, that the Germans never found. Some guys who knew how to make a radio would trade American cigarettes with the German guards for all the different parts they needed to make a radio—a secret radio. They got it working and would listen to the BBC. Somebody would type the news down on a piece of paper and we would pass it around after dark and read by those oleo lights. Just one copy passed around."

Below, the January 18, 1945 issue of the prisoners' daily underground newspaper, typed from BBC news heard on their secret radio. Notice the "Powwow" logo at the top.

Liberation by the Russians at the End of the War

"We were in that prison camp for nine months. We were liberated by Russians before the war was over. They reached us first. They were a drunken mob. We knew that the Russians were only a day's march away from us. The Germans guards left the towers and put American officers in the towers. We knew the Russians were coming because the Germans were burning all the records. Our senior officers told us the safest thing was to stay where we were. The Russians who came would push their sleeves up and show us a half-dozen watches up their arms. They wanted to sell them to us. 'Take your pick', they said. They had stolen them from the German people. They would say, 'Schnapps. Ya, ya!' They were wild."

189

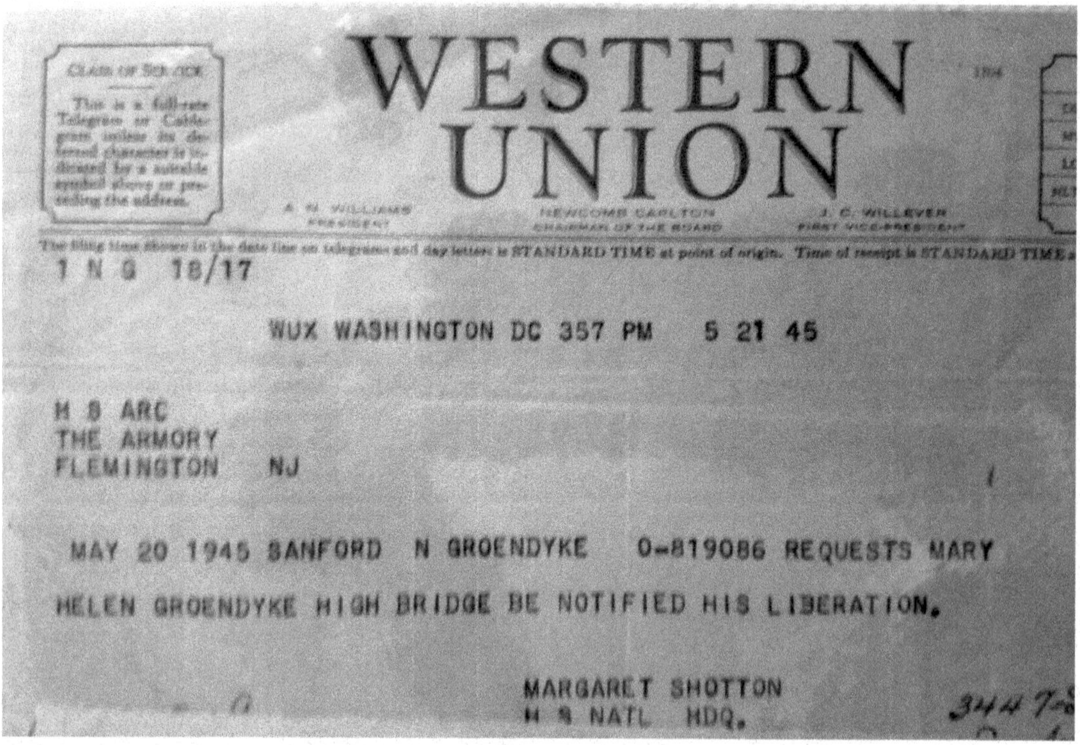
WESTERN UNION

A. N. WILLIAMS, PRESIDENT — NEWCOMB CARLTON, CHAIRMAN OF THE BOARD — J. C. WILLEVER, FIRST VICE-PRESIDENT

The filing time shown in the date line on telegrams and day letters is STANDARD TIME at point of origin. Time of receipt is STANDARD TIME

1 N G 18/17

WUX WASHINGTON DC 357 PM 5 21 45

H S ARC
THE ARMORY
FLEMINGTON NJ

MAY 20 1945 SANFORD N GROENDYKE 0-819086 REQUESTS MARY HELEN GROENDYKE HIGH BRIDGE BE NOTIFIED HIS LIBERATION.

MARGARET SHOTTON
H S NATL HDQ.

Above, the much hoped-for telegram to Mary Helen Groendyke reads:

"Darling well and safe love Sandy Groendyke"

Waiting in France to Go Home

"There was a small airport there. So in three or four days we flew out to France. They flew us across the Ruhr Valley and we saw the Cologne Cathedral. It was the only thing left standing around there. They took us to Camp Lucky Strike. It was in Normandy where the troops come in during the D-Day landing. We found out that it would be a month before we could leave. There were so many they had to get back. There weren't enough boats."

"A buddy of mine and I said, 'Let's go to Paris.' But we couldn't get a pass for Paris. They weren't letting Americans go there because they had such a food shortage in Paris. So we just asked for a weekend pass and got it. Then we went out and hitched a ride with a truck heading that way. When the truck stopped, we didn't know if it would be MPs who were looking for guys like us and might arrest us for being AWOL. Turned out they were guys doing the same thing we were doing—sneaking off to Paris. They told us they go to Paris every weekend. So we got the right truck!"

AWOL in Paris

"One of the guys in the truck said, 'Where are you staying in Paris? How are you going to get around?' We didn't know. They said, 'You can stay where we're staying.' When we got there, they stopped in the outskirts of Paris. We all got on the underground. I guess military got to ride free.

"When we came out of the underground in Paris, we were right under the Arc de Triomphe, right in the middle of town. We were so lucky. The other guys walked us over a few blocks to the place they were staying. One went inside and asked if we could stay there. He came back and said we could stay. We went in and realized it was a whorehouse. The guy introduced us to the Madam. We had something to eat and then the girls magically came out and we had a party. We had just come out of a German prison camp and now we were partying with girls in Paris. We didn't care. We couldn't go into the restaurants because the MPs had orders not to let American soldiers in. But the Red Cross had coffee and donuts they gave us for free. They had stands all over Paris. A lot of people were doing the same thing we were doing. So we lived on coffee and donuts three meals a day.

"Then we met a guy there at the donut stand who asked if we wanted to get some food. He said the 'wheels' had taken over the biggest club in Paris, and the officers' club was a restaurant. But he knew there was a guard who didn't enforce the rule about not admitting enlisted men. We went to that restaurant at that time and got in with no trouble. So we went back at the same time most days and had a good meal.

"The Red Cross had a place downtown where you could get free tickets for everything. We got Folies Bergere, Versailles, the Louvre, and a couple of shows. If you were wearing a uniform, you were king. Eventually we got tired of all this luxury and decided to go back to Camp Lucky Strike. I tell you I've had a good life. So when we got back the officer dressed us up and down and said he could court martial us. He thought a minute and said, 'Oh, hell. Forget it. I'd do the same thing!'"

The "Aviators' Dollar Bill" pictured above was carried by pilots to get a "Short Snort" for free. Pilots signed each other's dollar bills. The tradition was that if a pilot didn't have his "Aviators' Dollar Bill" with him, he had to buy drinks for all the other pilots.

On the right, above, is Sandy's pilot's license.

Coming Home

"Finally we caught a slow boat, one of these concrete things and spent eight days getting across the ocean. But they did have food on there. We docked in Virginia. I called my dad and he was, of course, overjoyed. Then I called the home of my wife, Mary Helen's mother in New Jersey. Mary Helen had no idea when I would be home, so she had gone to Washington, D.C. to visit a girlfriend of hers. Her mother gave me the friend's phone number. I called her and of course, we got together in D.C. as soon as possible. It was on the mainline, only an hour away. It was great that I had arrived in Virginia, so close to where Mary Helen was that weekend. We had a wonderful time."

Back in the States After the War

"We stayed at my father's place in High Bridge, New Jersey, (photo above) for a while. I stayed in the service and was transferred to Florida. I always wanted to work in Denver. It was known as the country club of the air. I asked for a transfer to Denver and got it. For a pilot, that was heaven. Mary Helen had her degree and worked as a teacher. Our daughter, Sandra, was born there. My dad wanted me to get out of the service and come to New Jersey and work with him in his business. He was ready to turn the business over to me. But I loved flying and stayed in. Eventually, I went back and joined my dad's business, which was real estate and insurance. Over the years, I specialized more in insurance. Dad died after one and one-half years. In addition, I also served as the New Jersey State Inheritance Tax Supervisor. The people I met in Rotary were most helpful in civilian life.

Mary Helen and I also had a son, Tom. Sadly, Mary Helen passed away in 2007. We moved to North Carolina when we retired in 1986."

Sandy Groendyke is pictured in 2019 in his home in Columbus, N.C. with portraits of his son, Tom, and daughter, Sandra.

O.E. Starnes, Jr., U.S. Army

Corporal O.E. Starnes, Jr., in Belgium, 1943

O.E. (Oscar Edwin) Starnes, Jr. joined the U.S. Army in 1943 at age 19, served in Italy, Belgium, France, and Germany, and was discharged in 1946. He earned the Purple Heart.

In the Army

In 1943, Asheville native O.E. Starnes, Jr. was in his second year at Davidson College, in North Carolina, when he decided to join the U.S. Army. His story begins: "I trained in Texas and then boarded a ship with thousands of other soldiers bound for Italy. I was made a machine gunner.

"We put three pegs on the ground to hold the machine gun in place. The bullets were looped into a cord that fed into the machine gun. The German airplanes were flying over. We had gunners on the ground that were shooting back at them and firing mortars. We moved north and up into Belgium. We were digging holes, hiding behind trees, doing the best we could to return fire.

"On May 3, 1945, I turned 21. I was carrying some ammunition back up to my machine gun. In each hand I had a metal satchel. I peeked out to where my gun was. The Germans must have seen me. I got shot across the top of my head. It took out hair, hide, skin, and bled heavily. But it didn't crack my skull. The good Lord saved me from any terrible injury. It knocked me down and somebody else eventually came and got the ammunition that I was carrying and took it up to the gun. My sergeant got shot too, just like I did. They took us back to the hospital. I recovered OK.

"I was there for 2½ years when the fighting began to wind down. We were in Belgium when the Germans surrendered. We thought we were going to have to go to Japan, but the U.S. dropped the bombs, the Japanese surrendered, and that war was over."

O.E. Starnes, Jr. on the far right, with two buddies in Belgium

After the War

"In April of 1946 I was discharged. I went back and finished college on the G.I. Bill, then went to law school at U.N.C. Chapel Hill. I met Sarah Jane Whitmire, who was a school teacher. We were married, built a little house in Asheville, and had three children, O.E., III (who sadly died at age 43), Amy, and Jane. Sadly, Sarah Jane passed away in 1976 after we had been married for 29 years.

"I practiced law in Asheville and traveled around, often representing insurance companies and physicians, until my retirement in 2015. I enjoyed snow skiing, tennis, water sports, and playing clarinet in a Dixieland band. I also sang with a barbershop quartet with the SPEBSQSA, Inc. That means, 'Society for the Preservation and Encouragement of Barber Shop Quartet Singing in America.'

At right: O.E., Sarah Jane, and their children were featured in the Saturday Evening Post magazine as they dined at Howard Johnson's Restaurant in Asheville, N.C.

"I married Lida, a widow who had four children. We were married 38 years, but she sadly passed away in 2016. I'm close to my children, stepchildren, grandchildren, and six great-grandchildren. I've been very lucky with my wonderful wives. Of course, they were lucky to have me, too," O.E. teased. "All in all, I'm a very blessed man."

At right: O.E. and his second wife, Lida. She passed away in 2016.

Above, O.E. Starnes, Jr.'s insignia and medals.

Below, his Purple Heart.

P-47 Pilot Ed Cottrell, U.S, Army Air Corps

2nd Lt. Edwin Cottrell

Edwin Cottrell served in the Army Air Corps from August 1942 through 1945, then enlisted in the Air Force Reserves in 1950 and completed 28 years.

His father, Dr. Elmer Cottrell, served in the U.S. Army in World War I. His father-in-law, Dr. Paul Weed was wounded and received two Purple Hearts serving in the U.S. Army in World War I.

On April 3, 2020 at age 98, Ed Cottrell told his story:

"I was born in Oklahoma City, Oklahoma, on January 17, 1922. When I was six months old, my father and mother moved the family to Slippery Rock, Pennsylvania, where he was a teacher at Slippery Rock Normal School, which later became Slippery Rock Teachers College, which later became Slippery Rock University. I grew up and went to elementary school, junior high school, high school, and college in Slippery Rock.

"While I was in college, I met my wife, Millie, while we were freshmen. We went together all through college. Before I went overseas, we got married."

I Wanted to Be a Pilot

"My military career actually started in the summer of my sophomore year. The government offered any students interested in getting a pilot's license to enroll in their CPT (college pilot training) program, which I did. I went to Sharon, Pennsylvania, and got 30 hours in a Piper Cub. I got my pilot's license during the summer between my sophomore and junior year.

"Pearl Harbor took place and in August 1942 I got my draft notice that I was going to be called very shortly. I decided I wanted to be a pilot, so I went to Pittsburgh, 52 miles south of Slippery Rock. I took the Navy test and passed it, the Army Air Corps test and passed it. The Navy said, 'If you join us, you'll leave tomorrow.' The Army Air Corps said 'We're not ready for you yet. If you join us, go back to school and we'll call you.' So that being a no-brainer, I decided to go with the Army Air Corps.

"I went back to school in the fall of '42. In February of '43, I got a notice that I was to report to Miami Beach. I got aboard a train in Pittsburgh with maybe 300 to 400 other potential cadets and we arrived in Miami Beach where we did a month of basic training.

"From there I was sent to a college in Beloit, Wisconsin, for two more months of sort of basic training—a lot of physical training and radio work. Since I had just about graduated with a degree in physical education, they said, 'Why don't you run our physical training program?' which I did.

"When we left Beloit, we were assigned to Santa Ana, California, where there were maybe 30 or 40 squadrons with over 100 people in each squadron. We did lots of drills and lots of PT. I was assigned to flight school at Visalia, California, where I went to train in a PT-19. During that time, they taught us lots of discipline, lots of flying, and lots of marching—PT and marching. During that time, you learned basically what the Army expected of you.

"I finished flight school primary training and was sent to Chico, California for basic. There I flew the Vultee Vibrator, the PT-13, which was really a good airplane to get basic training in. It had wide landing gears and it shook all over, but it was a very reliable plane. From there we started to do aerobatics and we did a lot of landings and take-offs on short landing strips. We did some radio work.

"While we were at Chico, we were to choose the area of the Army Air Corps we wanted to expand our training, whether it be bombers or fighters. So I chose to go to fighters and was assigned to Luke Field in Phoenix, Arizona for my advanced training. I flew the AT-6, the Texan, which is a great little aircraft still used today as a starter plane for Air Force pilots going into their flight school.

"At the end of my training at Luke Field, the last two weeks we had five hours of flying in the P-40 Fighter. That's the fighter that we thought we were all going to be assigned to overseas. Upon graduation as a 2nd LT, I went back to Slippery Rock. There Millie and I got married and spent two weeks together before I was to report to Wendover Field in Utah.

"Then I went to Wendover Field for my indoctrination to the plane I was going to fly overseas. At Wendover, I was going to find out which theatre of operation where I would be assigned. We got to Wendover and there I found the most beautiful aircraft I'd seen—a brand new P-47 Thunderbolt.

"When I saw that, I knew pretty much that we were going to the European theatre of operation where we'd be working with the Army in close support. And that's exactly what happened. At Wendover Field, we got a lot of aerial gunnery experience, we did a lot of night flying, we did a lot of formation flying, did a lot of dive-bombing and strafing runs—just as if we were in actual combat.

"After six weeks, I was assigned to go to Baton Rouge, Louisiana on the way to New York to embark towards Europe. In August of 1944, I was put aboard a beautiful cruise ship called the Isle de France, which was now a troop ship. We were assigned two people to a room, which meant that one slept during the day and one slept at night till we got to England."

Above, pilots of the 493rd Fighter Squadron
Ed Cottrell is kneeling at far right, partially behind another pilot.

In Europe Flying the P-47

"We were in England about a week and I was assigned with a lot of my friends I trained with at Wendover—to the 48th Fighter Group, 493rd Fighter Squadron, which was at an airfield called Cambrai, located outside of Paris. We got our induction to become members of the 493rd Fighter Squadron. The second day we were there, we were taken up to formation with one of the pilots who was a veteran. We flew formation and did some dive-bombing attacks and strafing attacks without firing guns—just so we got an idea of what we were going to be doing.

"While at Cambrai we started to fly our missions and then in late September we moved to St. Trond, Belgium. It was a beautiful airfield. There were 10,000-foot runways and there were three squadrons of the 48th Fighter Group based around the airfield. We were on one side and the 492nd and the 494th were on the other side. We were there from September until the middle of January. I'll tell you about three incidents that happened while we were at St. Trond.

"On December 6th, the weather was very bad. The 9th Army was in close pursuit of the German military. We were called on a very, very rainy, cloudy day with no more than 200 feet visibility, to go skip-bomb a soccer field where the Americans were on one side and the Germans were on the other side. It was pretty much a stalemate.

"I flew wing man to our squadron commander, Major Latiolais, that day. He led 12 of us on this mission where we were no more than 200 feet above the ground, flying at over 300 miles an hour, until we came to the little town of Jullich, Germany. We were required to come in over the American troops, maybe 30 or 40 yards across the field to skip-bomb the Germans on the other side. We made two or three passes, got a lot of ground fire, and were successful in dropping our bombs. The Americans were able to move forward and push the Germans back.

"Upon returning to our base we found out that almost every plane had a lot of bullet holes in it where the small ground fire had hit the planes. The P-47 was such a good plane, that didn't faze it at all. Our 493rd Fighter Squadron got the Presidential Citation for that operation. Major Latiolais did a tremendous job of leading us on that mission, where some of the time we were on instruments and some of the time actually at treetop level."

Close Encounter with ME-109s

"On December 17th we were on a mission to locate some tiger tanks which were just east of Cologne in a wooded area, on their way to Bastogne. We found out the Germans had broken through and the Battle of the Bulge was taking place. Our airfield was the closest to the Battle of the Bulge—Bastogne.

"Again, I was flying wing to our commander. We located the tiger tanks in the woods and went down on a dive-bombing mission. Major Latiolais was the first plane down. I was the second plane down. We dropped our bombs. As we pulled up, we ran into a group of ME-109 German Luftwaffe planes.

"On our pullout, on our way up, I noticed an ME [Messerschmitt]-109 coming down at one o'clock toward my squadron commander. I called to him that there was a bandit at one o'clock. The 109 shifted a little bit and the next thing I knew I felt this big blast and a 20mm cannon apparently hit my plane. All of a sudden, there was oil all over the windshield and I couldn't see anything. I was on an upward slope.

"I opened the canopy, got on the radio to my commander and said I'd been hit and was heading west and going to fly the plane as far as I could. The plane sort of kicked out but it chugged along at about 120 miles an hour with oil flying out all over my windshield.

"I looked out on one side and there was a German 109. I looked out on the other side and there was another 109. They crisscrossed behind me and I thought I was going to be shot down. But they came up and pulled in right next to me. They flew with me back to the bomb line where they used their thumbs and first fingers to make a little circle and peeled off. That was the signal they were leaving me, 'Good luck and God bless' without shooting me down.

"I kept going. I had no idea where I was. My radio still worked. I asked anybody that could hear if they knew where A-92 field was. A voice on the radio said, 'You're not very far from it. Turn 90 degrees and you should run into it.'

"I found out I was south of the airfield. It was strange territory because we never landed at A-92 except when we came in from the north. Just as my plane was ready to touch down at the airfield, the engine froze over. I had to make a dead-stick landing and rolled to a stop."

I Kissed the Ground

"When I got out of that plane, I kissed the ground because I was a very fortunate person. I could've been shot down. The engine could've quit. A lot of things could've happened. But I came out the best anyone could have in that situation.

"I lost one of my roommates that day, 2nd Lt. Art Sommers. He was a graduate of the University of Southern California. He got shot down. I didn't see him go down, but he didn't come back from the mission. We found out later that they found his plane and he had been killed."

Battle of the Bulge

"On New Year's Day, 1945, right during the Battle of the Bulge, the Germans had surrounded Bastogne. We were 17 miles away from there. We had been told that if the Germans broke through, we would probably be prisoners of war.

"The day before New Year's Day we were told all but 12 of the planes would be flown out to another airfield. They were going to leave 12 planes with 12 pilots. The 12 pilots were going to be the least experienced ones. So on New Year's Eve, we were told to get rid of all our personal items—burn them and keep only what we needed—our dog tags. No pictures.

"We went to bed. At four o'clock in the morning I was told to get up; I was going to be the lead pilot on runway alert. Runway alert is nothing more than four planes at the end of the runway, engines running. If the radar picked up any incoming, we were able to take off and go intercept them."

The Germans Hated Our B-17s and B-24s

"Without warning, eight Focke-Wulf 190s came in at ground level, below the radar, and came right over where we were sitting, to the middle of our airfield. There was a B-17 that was burned out and a B-24 that was burned out. They were sitting there waiting to be scrapped. The Germans didn't know that, of course. The Germans hated B-17s and B-24s because those were the planes that were bombing all their factories.

"The FW-190s went right to that B-24 and B-17 with their machine guns going. But they didn't drop their belly tanks. As they came to the end of the field and pulled up to make another pass, our anti-aircraft guns hit most of the 190s. Two of them were not hit and they came around to make another pass. The first of the 190s was on his dive down. He kept going down and down. He didn't pull out and he crashed at the end of the runway. The other plane kept going and shooting at the B-24 and the B-17.

"We went out to where the pilot was lying with his plane in flames and found out that he had a bullet in the middle of his forehead. He didn't look to be any more than 17 years old. We found out later that all the American airfields up and down the bomb line were hit at the same time that day. The German Luftwaffe took a tremendous loss.

"On that day when I was on runway alert, our squadron went on a mission. Another of my best friends and roommate was shot down and killed. His name was 2nd Lt. Ted Smith, from Wenatchee, Washington.

"From January 1 on, our biggest concern in any missions that we had, was the flak that came from the anti-aircraft gun and the small arms fire from the people that we were dive-bombing and strafing.

"The German air force, what was left of it, was primarily used to attack our bombers that were used to bomb the factories all over Germany.

"The Americans broke through then and got the Germans retreating from Bastogne. Starting in the middle of January, the 9th Army, which we supported, was in the north. They started pushing the Germans back. Every mission we flew was in support of the 9th Army, either dive-bombing or strafing, or whatever they needed.

"As the 9ᵗʰ Army moved, we moved from then until May. We took off and landed on metal strips that the engineers put down in farm fields that were level. When we landed, the mud would come up between the metal strips. We had very short runways. When we were ready to move, thee engineers took those metal strips and moved them up to the next area.

"We just lived out of houses right near the airfield, wherever there was anything available for sleeping. They were empty either because people had fled from the Germans, or the Germans had lived in them and they left. A lot of Jewish people were herded away and killed, as you know. There were a lot of empty houses. Some of them had holes in the roofs. Some had no damage. But wherever we could find an empty house, that's where we bedded down."

The War in Europe Ended

"We never did establish a base from January until May. Then in May, the 48ᵗʰ was down below Munich. I flew my last mission, my 65ᵗʰ mission, out of Nuremberg. Then the war was over in June. Those people who had 65 or more missions, if they wanted to, could go home. If not, they would be going with the 48ᵗʰ Fighter Group which was going to Japan. I chose to go home because I had a little daughter that I hadn't seen.

"A couple of my buddies and I came home together. The other pilots left on a boat out of Antwerp to go to Japan. On their way, the war with Japan ended. I got home the 1ˢᵗ of July and had time at home before I went to San Antonio to be discharged on July 24."

At Home After the War

"I pursued a career in teaching and coaching: health and physical education, football, basketball, and baseball. While living in Beaver, Pennsylvania, I got my master's degree at University of Pittsburgh. I went to Penn State on a graduate assistantship, earning $145.00 a month. I also taught driver training, painted the school building, pumped gas, and delivered mail during the summers, anything to keep money coming in.

"I joined the Air Force Reserves to make a little extra money and still serve the country. When the Air Force Academy was being developed in Colorado Springs, I was assigned to go around to high schools and get kids interested in becoming cadets. I stayed in the reserves for 28 years and retired.

"I took a job in Hershey, Pennsylvania at Milton Hershey, at an orphan school for boys, as Director of Athletics. After three years, I went to West Chester State College where I taught swimming and classroom subjects, and coached tennis, football, baseball, and golf. Eventually I taught in the graduate school and became the Associate Dean. I did that until I retired at age 57.

"I had also worked for the National Golf Foundation, visiting schools promoting the game of golf. I started my own golf school, conducting golf clinics all over the world. I spent time in Holland, Japan, and all over the United States. I became friends with Jack Nicklaus, Greg Norman, Johnny Miller and many well-known golfers. I've had a great career.

"Millie and I lived in Florida and Pinehurst, N.C. before moving to Hendersonville. She had worked as a physical education, health, and dancing teacher in many schools over the years. She and I got to work at the same schools sometimes.

"We have two daughters, Carol and Susan. We're celebrating our 76th wedding anniversary on April 21, 2020."

Talking About the War

About the years after World War II, Cottrell said, "For a long time, I didn't talk about the war. I wanted to forget it. Then about 15 years ago, at one of our squadron reunions, we talked about how the country was different now.

"Someone said, 'We never talked about our military experience, but maybe we need to, because this country needs to get back to what it was back during World War II, when the country was in trouble and everybody pitched in. There was no bickering and no questions about what we were going to do.'

"If you weren't able to join the fighting, you worked in the factories. You took care of helping each other out. You did rationing, whatever was needed, to make sure the United States survived.

"So at that reunion, we all said that if we were ever asked, we would talk about our military experiences. That's why I talk about what we went through in order to preserve the freedom of this country, to keep us from speaking German or Japanese. If Hitler had been successful, he wouldn't have stopped at anything. Thank the Lord we stopped him."

When Ed Cottrell received a Quilt of Valor in a March 7, 2000 ceremony (photo at right), he dedicated his quilt to four people:

To his father and father-in-law (recipient of two Purple Hearts), both WWI veterans.

And to Ed's two pilot friends and roommates, who were shot down and did not survive: 2nd Lt. Ted Smith and 2nd Lt. Art Sommers.

211

At right, Ed Cottrell (standing at left) with WWII veterans Harold Wellington (also standing) and George Sarros (seated), on a visit to the Veterans History Museum of the Carolinas on March 4, 2020.

THE WAR IN THE PACIFIC

FOLLOWING ARE THE PERSONAL STORIES
OF VETERANS
WHO SERVED IN THE PACIFIC

Larry Johns, U.S. Army Air Corps

1ˢᵗ Lt. Larry Johns, Navigator, U.S. Army Air Corps

Latimer (Larry) Dexter Johns served in the Pacific as a navigator in the U.S. Army Air Corps. He served in the Army from 1941-1945.

A Father's Tales of the North Pacific

by Michel Johns Robertson

My father, Latimer Dexter "Larry" Johns, served in the Pacific during WWII as a navigator in the Army Air Corps, flying B-29 bombing missions from Guam to targets on mainland Japan. Years later, when my sister and I asked about the war, he shared only those stories he deemed appropriate for his young daughters' ears. The following stories are my childhood favorites.

Floating High in the Texas Sky

On December 7, 1941, Larry and a high school buddy were en route to Los Angeles from their hometown in Wisconsin, hired by a local auto dealer to drive the vehicle to the west coast. Their plan was to enjoy the California beaches and eventually hitchhike home to the wintry Midwest. They scrapped their plans when they learned of the attack on Pearl Harbor, agreeing to hitchhike home immediately to join the army.

Larry was assigned to the Army Air Corps as a navigator and attended flight school in Texas. On one eventful flight, the plane's engine caught fire, necessitating that the crew bail out. Larry described the experience of parachuting through the sky, each *whoosh* of wind wafting him from side to side. When I asked him what he was thinking as he headed towards earth, he answered truthfully. "All I could think of was, 'I want my mother.'"

Larry landed in a yard where an elderly woman was hanging her laundry. She looked at him wide-eyed as he plunked down nearby. "Did you jump from that plane?" she asked him. "No ma'am," Larry replied. "I was sent from heaven."

Peaches and Pasta

Larry had a healthy appetite and consumed with gusto everything my mother prepared, with two exceptions. Before they married, he warned her that there were two dishes he never wanted to see on his table: canned peaches and macaroni-and-cheese, Guam's K-rations. "They kept us alive," he grumbled. "That's all I'll say about them."

At right, Larry with his dog, Jenny (around 1974)

Toads in the Roads

During Guam's rainy season, heavy military traffic created deep furrows in the dirt roads which quickly filled with muddy water. At night, as Jeeps sloshed along the rutted roads, their headlights illuminated thousands of frenzied giant cane toads leaping to safety from their watery troughs.

Fright Night

In Guam's tropical, insect-infested climate, mosquito netting over the beds was a must. One lucky day, Larry received a large block of Wisconsin cheddar cheese from his mother. To protect this culinary treasure from insects, he hung it inside the netting from a rope over his cot, tied to the reinforcing pole. Awakened by a scrabbling noise from above, Larry gaped in horror at an enormous rat hanging over his head, clinging to the block of cheese and gnawing on Wisconsin's finest cheddar.

In his struggle to escape, Larry fell out of bed, and he and the panicked rat struggled in the netted prison until the rodent finally escaped. Hyperventilating, Larry collapsed on his cot. He never revealed whether he finished the block of cheese.

Redemption

After the war, Larry married my mother and the couple moved to Detroit where he attended night school on the GI Bill at Wayne State University. After school on a rainy night, he noticed a young Japanese woman from his class, struggling with her umbrella against the cold winter wind. His invitation to her to share his cab was readily accepted. During the ride, the conversation turned to the war. The young woman told Larry the story of her Japanese village.

"On a rainy evening like tonight, air raid sirens woke my village. As on so many other occasions, we rushed to our shelters. But this night was different. The planes didn't drop their bombs -- they flew over our village and disappeared into the dark sky. We were joyful as we returned to our homes.

"Suddenly, out of the fog, the planes returned, dropping their bombs on our village and the people in their beds. Many died. It was the worst night of the war."

Larry listened in stunned silence. He recognized the village and the night—it was *his* squadron that had flown this mission. In the fog and clouds, they had missed the town. Correcting their error, they turned and made a second pass, catching the villagers off guard.

217

The woman listened wordlessly to Larry's confession, not speaking for the rest of the trip.

She was absent for several nights, and Larry experienced guilt and concern that his admission had caused her to drop the course. Then, one evening, he saw her sitting in the front row. After the lecture, he left quickly, not wanting to cause her additional pain.

As he hurried toward home, Larry heard her calling, "Mr. Johns! Wait!" Catching up to him, she shyly presented a parcel wrapped in brown paper. Unwrapping it revealed a beautiful hand-knit wool scarf. "You were very kind to me," she explained. "I knitted this for you. Mr. Johns, our war is over."

My father wore the scarf every winter for the rest of his life.

Above, the Johns family at the golf course. From left, Larry, Leslie, Michel, and Pat.

Frank Davis, U.S. Navy Reserve

Ensign Frank Davis, U.S. Navy Reserve

Frank Davis, born in Hobart, Indiana in 1916, joined the U.S. Navy Reserve on March 17, 1942. He served until June, 1945.

"We were at war."

When asked, "Why did you volunteer for the military?" Frank Davis said, "We were at war. All men lined up to enlist. It was the thing to do." His answer demonstrates his feeling of personal responsibility and patriotism and for the culture at the time. Frank said, "I was in the car with my mother on December 7, 1941, when we heard about the Japanese bombing Pearl Harbor. We both felt disbelief.

"I had graduated from college with a degree in journalism and had been working for a local weekly newspaper in Hobart, Indiana. Later I worked for a syndicated newspaper in Chicago. My father became ill and did not recover well, so I had quit my job in Chicago and went home to help take care of my father.

"After my father died, I had to beat the bushes to find work. I was 26 and working at the local draft board when I tried to join the Navy. They told me I had two bad wisdom teeth. I went to the dentist and had them extracted the next day, went back to the Chicago recruiting office, and they accepted me on March 17, 1942. I had to make my peace with my decision. I had only been married for nine months to my wife Mary and I had partial responsibility for supporting my widowed mother."

In the Navy

"They assigned me to serve at the Office of Naval Officer Procurement at the Board of Trade Building in Chicago. When I reported to the office, as Yeoman Second Class, I saw a complete floor of seamen. There must have been 50 or 60 of them on typewriters, processing applications for commissions in the Naval Reserve. To my amazement, I was assigned as yeoman to the executive officer. I think it was because I had a college degree. Also, way back in high school, I had learned stenography. Although I wasn't an expert, I could take dictation. I spent a year as the yeoman to the executive officer of the Naval Office of Procurement.

"Most of the men working there were unrated seamen, but one of my particular pleasures was doing an errand out on the floor where all these men were working. When they saw me coming, everything would get quiet. They would start working hard. It gave me an edge of prestige I've never enjoyed before or since," he joked.

"I was by myself in the executive office. The captain of the entire crew would be sitting in his adjacent office eating chocolates most of the time. We'd handle correspondence. After a little more than a year, Colonel Clarkson said to me, 'You know, Davis, you ought to be an officer. I'm going to recommend you for a commission.' Well, I was stunned, but I wasn't going to protest, of course. Immediately my commission came back as an ensign.

At left, Ensign Davis in San Diego

220

"My first duty was at Harvard University. There were several different naval schools at Harvard during this time. I was assigned to the communications office and I learned Morse Code, how to read flag signals, signal lights, and everything about communication. But the most secret thing was the encoding machines. Highly secret. We didn't even acknowledge that such a thing existed. That also meant learning how to decode messages.

"My first assignment was destroyer school in Norfolk, Virginia, learning the ins and outs of serving on a destroyer. From there I was sent to San Francisco, where a crew was being

assembled for a new destroyer under construction in the Bremerton shipyard in Washington State. My crew was being trained in San Francisco on Treasure Island. This new destroyer was the *U.S.S. Morrison DDS-560*. We took our gunnery training on an island near San Diego. Some poor island there—we probably battered it to pieces.

Frank's wife Mary (at left) was sometimes able to visit him while he was stationed in California. (This picture was taken just moments before Mary was doused by a rogue wave!)

"We all got on a train to go to Seattle where the ship was built and commissioned, but still needed to be outfitted. We were the crew. The ship was painted in camouflage. It was also desensitized (demagnetized) by wrapping a degaussing cable all around the ship. [The cable was later removed.] All the crew members were cautioned to take off our watches and jewelry, because they would be affected by this demagnetizing process. [Degaussing reduced or eliminated the magnetic field of the destroyer to prevent the Japanese naval magnetic mines from being pulled to the ship. Gauss is a unit of magnetism, named for Carl Friedrich Gauss, a German mathematician.]

"The night before we were to depart for Bremerton, someone brought aboard a case of the mumps, which spread through the ship. Two out of every three people came down with the mumps. I had had the mumps as a child, so I had to do triple duty in the code room to cover for the two who were sick. I also had to keep doing my watches on board the ship. This went on for several days. I was whipped, having no sleep. I became ill, was hospitalized, and transported to the Naval hospital in Bremerton. I was carried off that ship unconscious. I don't know how long I was unconscious or sleeping, but when I finally woke up, I had grown quite a beard, so it must have been a long time. When I was finally able to get out of bed, I looked out the window and there went my ship, the *Morrison,* sailing away.

"I was transferred to another hospital, where I was in rehabilitation for another month. I wasn't able to recover for sea duty, and was reassigned to work in the code room in Naval Headquarters, in San Diego. One day I typed a coded message that we were receiving. When it [automatically] came out in English, I could see that the *USS Morrison* had been sunk in the Battle of Okinawa. It had taken four kamikaze strikes to put that ship down. It was my job to report that news to the captain of the facility. Below, a stock photo of the U.S.S. Morrison, which on May 4, 1945, was sunk by four Japanese kamikazes.

"Many of the crew were picked up by rescue ships, for which I'm grateful. If I hadn't been sick, I would have been on that ship, and maybe not here today.

"Then it was 1945 and it appeared that the war was winding down. They were offering discharges to nonessential staff. I was discharged under honorable circumstances and came home in June of 1945. The war was over August 6.

August 11, 1945 edition from Frank Davis' collection of historic newspapers

"When I came home, my in-laws, who were in the construction business, were desperate for help. All the available help was in the military. They put me to work as an accountant for their business and that was the end of my journalism career. My wife Mary and I had two daughters. I continued handling the books for the construction business until I was 54 years old.

Mary and Frank Davis with daughters
Chris and Alison in the 1950s

"Visiting some friends who lived in Franklin, North Carolina, I came down with 'North Carolina-itis'. Mary and I discovered Cedar Mountain and moved here in 1970. I had thought I would open my own accounting business, but I found that I really enjoyed sleeping in, and that cured me! Fortunately, we were able to enjoy retirement early. Unfortunately, Mary only lived six years after that.

"I discovered I enjoyed riding motorcycles and continued acquiring bigger and bigger ones, riding until I was in my eighties."

Wearing his commemorative USS Morrison cap, Frank Davis is shown in his Cedar Mountain, N.C., home in 2016 with his grandson, Dan Flinn, and his daughter, Alison McFadden.

Gattis Ervin Allen, U.S. Navy

Gattis Ervin "G.E." Allen, Motor Machinist Mate First Class, U.S Navy, 1942

G.E. Allen joined the U.S. Navy with two of his brothers after the Japanese attacked Pearl Harbor. He served in New Guinea, New Zealand, and Australia. He was discharged in 1945.

G.E. passed away in 1997. These stories were told to and written for Janis Allen about her father by her mother Pauline Allen. (Pauline died in 2003.)

Growing Up in the Mountains and Foothills

Gattis Ervin Allen was born May 1, 1911, in Madison County, North Carolina, one of 11 children. He completed the fourth grade and went to work at Whitney Mill at age 14 to help support his family after his family moved to South Carolina. Later at Henrietta Mills Company, he became a supervisor when he was twenty, working his way up from sweeper.

Some people at the mill called him "Gat," short for Gattis, but he also liked to be called by his initials, G.E. When General Electric began to use GE to label its products, he jokingly referred to his name as General Electric. He always bought GE appliances after that. Later, when Ronald Reagan became the TV spokesman for GE and was making speeches about patriotism and free-market capitalism around the country, his admiration for the future president began.

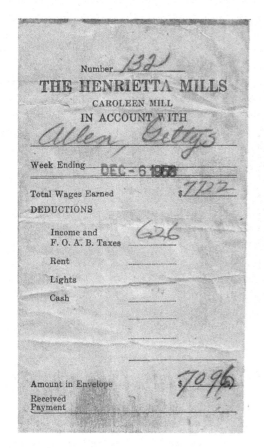

This pay stub came in an envelope with cash. (His first name was misspelled, but the cash worked just fine!)

The War in the Pacific

When the Japanese bombed Pearl Harbor in 1941, G.E.'s niece Dot Rice (age 11 at the time) remembers the family gathering at her Aunt Anne's house in Caroleen, N.C., listening to the radio, feeling angry and some people crying.

CAROLEEN BROTHERS IN ARMED SERVICE

JOHN L. ALLEN · GATTIS E. ALLEN · CHARLIE E. ALLEN

Shown above are three sons of Mrs. Hattie Allen of Caroleen, who are in the armed forces of the nation. John L. Allen, in the U. S. Navy, is stationed at Long Island, N. Y. Gattis E. Allen, also of the Navy, is somewhere in the Southwest Pacific area. Charlie E. Allen, enlisted June 7, 1942, is also in the Southwest Pacific area.

THREE FOREST CITY BROTHERS IN MARINES

PVT. FRANK RICE · PFC. J. P. RICE · PFC. CLYDE E. RICE

Shown here are three brothers, all sons of Mr. and Mrs. P. B. Rice of Forest City, who are serving the nation as Marines. Pfc. Clyde E. Rice enlisted in the Marine Corps September 3, 1942, and is now overseas. Pfc. J. P. Rice enlisted in the Marine Corps December 14, 1941 and is now stationed in Florida. Pvt. Frank H. Rice entered the Marine Corps September 1942, and is now overseas.

G.E.'s nephew, J.P. Rice, (bottom, center in the newspaper photo at left) was the first that night to say he was quitting his job at the mill to join the Marines. His brothers Frank and Clyde also joined the Marines. They're pictured on either side of J.P. (Unfortunately, their names were erroneously reversed.) The three Allen brothers (top row) John, G.E., and Charles joined the service together.

G.E.'s wife Pauline remembered, "There was a big rally in Charlotte on the day the Navy inducted hundreds of recruits. We went to see our boys off with hundreds of others, and joined in the street party. They had speeches, music, food, dancing, and hotel rooms paid for by the Navy.

"Near the end of the war, G.E. was stationed in Norfolk," Pauline said. "I went and stayed with him there for over a year until he got out. Boy, it was a noisy time up there on V.E. Day [Victory in Europe Day] and on the day Roosevelt died and on V.J. Day [Victory Over Japan]. All the stores and cafes and everything closed, but the churches rung their bells all day and kept their doors open for people to come in and pray."

From left: Brothers G.E., Charles, and John joined the Navy on the same day.

G.E. kissing Pauline in a mountain setting, home on leave from the Navy

At right is sailor G.E. Allen's log while in the South Pacific in 1943. Note Nov. 15th entry at the bottom.

After G.E.'s funeral in 1997, his ship-mate, John Taylor, came to the house and told some stories about their time together in the war. They had both been motor machinist mates in the Navy.

John Taylor explained that during invasions of islands in the Pacific, his duty station was to man a machine gun on an LST landing craft. G.E.'s job was to feed the ammunition belt to the machine gun. They would fire at Japanese Zero fighter planes attacking them.

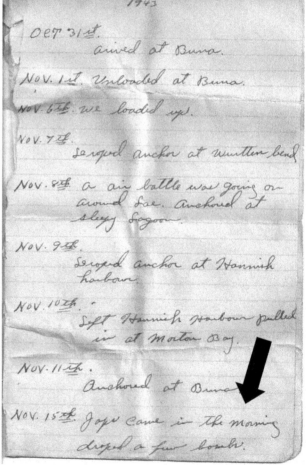

During one landing they fired at a Zero and thought they got him. It trailed smoke and crashed in the jungle. John made a note of where it went down. Later, after the island was safe, John got permission from the Skipper to go ashore and look for the Zero plane. He and G.E. took a hacksaw, went ashore, and found the plane. John explained that the propeller was made of Japanese aluminum which was softer than American-made aluminum.

They cut off the propeller, brought it back to their ship, and used the soft metal to make bracelets, rings, and other souvenirs. This replica of a P-38 American fighter plane is made from that aluminum. G.E. mounted a photo of his wife Pauline in the base as shown.

Two months before her death in 2003, G.E.'s wife Pauline wrote down a history of the war years. The following pages describe products made for service members at Caroleen Mill, where she worked during World War II.

11-25-02

Since we got onto
this old settlement
And the plants that
are operating for
the U.S. Government
making All the
merchendise the Armed
services Needs to carry
on the War to save
our "Dear Old Glory"
"and our good Home
land."
Well now comes The
Cotton means to
spinning the
products. They got
the raw Cotton from
Mississippi and the
other states that

grew cotton out in
the states that
grew cotton.
Then had to come
some way of
transporting the
products both
ways. So along
come the "steam
ships." On the
river near all
these plants,
delivering the raw
products and the
finished products.
The T-Shirts the
US government used
were the best in
the U S A. And they
sold the seconds in
all the General Stores

Love Letter from the War

The record pictured here contains an audio message G.E. sent to Pauline during the war (made while in port in California).

Transcript from G.E.'s recording:

G.E. Allen

Hello Pauline. This California is a fine place. Everything in the world to see. And I like this Navy more and more every day.

Don't you worry a bit about me. We shall come home victorious. We'll take care of 'em, all right.

God bless you and your sweet heart. And always remember me and I will you.

Tell Chester that I said he was a dear, sweet little boy and I'd like very much to see him. It's 3,400 miles between me and him. Tell Dot I said hello and tell Mother and all the rest I'll be seeing you soon.

Remember me always and all the things we've ever told each other. So long, Sugar . . . Darling. I love you, I love you.

Pauline Allen

After the War

Returning home after World War II, G.E., like many of his fellow servicemen, was full of optimism and gratitude for making it through alive. He was ready to build a life, a family, a career, a home. He returned to his job at Caroleen Mill, where he worked for 42 years until his retirement. He always had other businesses, including building houses, operating a fish camp, small engine repair, and an Amway distributorship.

At left is G.E. beside the log cabin home he and Pauline built in Sandy Mush, N.C..

G.E.'s hobby was restoring Model As and Model Ts. He's at right with a 1929 Model A Roadster with running boards and rumble seat. He's wearing a tie because his employer sent someone to take this photo for their company newsletter.

233

John L. Allen, U.S. Navy

John L. Allen, U.S. Navy

John Allen joined the Navy in 1942 and served in the Pacific until 1945.

John Allen was born in Marshall, North Carolina, in 1908. He was one of 11 children of Harriet Briggs Allen and Joby Allen. As a teenager, he moved with his family to Whitney, South Carolina, and worked in a cotton mill. Later he moved to Caroleen, N.C., to work in a cotton mill there. He later became a plumber and carpenter.

After the Japanese bombed Pearl Harbor, he and two brothers (John is at right in the picture here.) went together to Charlotte, N.C., and joined the Navy. He survived the sinking of three ships in the Pacific.

In 2009, Janis Allen asked her aunt, Bonnie Ruff Tate Allen, what her husband, John Allen (whom she married after the war), had told her about his time in the Navy. Following is Bonnie's letter telling John's story as he had told her. A typed version follows this handwritten letter.

Janis —
Trying to ans. your questions — first I can't write anymore — forgive —
It was 3 ships he had shot out from under him. He said it 3rd was the worst one. He was down in the engine room and something told him to get out of there. Said he run steps & climbed ladders to top deck. Said he had just got there when a Torpedo hit the ship and cut it half into. Said the engine room and all the bottom of the ship sank quickly. He got on a raft with 22 other sailors and drifted for 20 days. Most of them just give up and

3.

big day – they were all
set up down there for
a big event – Speakers
bands, recruiters + the
whole works – Me + Junk
and Zendia went down to
see them off – Honey was
already gone – Navy too –
I don't remember his ship
either. (Two wks later) will
try to get this in mail –
You got my job title wrong –
I was welder at N.S. Ship
building Co. Loved it – Women
were not allowed on ships.
We worked out on the "skid" –
We call it platform. Long +
no top over your head. In
winter we couldn't get on
enough clothes to stay warm.
Summer that sun was
really, really hot. Had to
wear coveralls + high top
shoes to keep the melting
steel off our skin –

Below is the typewritten version of Bonnie's letter:

Janis —

Trying to ans. your questions - first I can't write anymore — forgive —

It was 3 ships he had shot out from under him. He said 3rd was the worst one. He was down in the engine room and something told him to get out of there. Said he run steps and climbed ladders to top deck. Said he had just got there when a torpedo hit the ship and cut it half into. Said the engine room and all the bottom of the ship sank quickly. He got on a raft with 22 other sailors and drifted for 20 days. Most of them just give up and dropped off overboard.

Bonnie Ruff Allen

Said at one time a Jap sub came up and tried to get them to come on their sub but all refused. The Japs tossed them some sea rations and bid them farewell.

When he was rescued only 7 men were still on raft. He couldn't straighten his legs or walk — sitting in that position for so long — they flew him to Pocono Hospital for 30 days then gave him 30 days leave. I think Pocono Mts. or in N.Y. or Penn. I think he came out not long after that.

Do you remember about J.L. [John], G.E. and Chas all going to Char. and joining the Navy — was a big day — They were all set up down there for a big event — Speakers, bands, recruiters and the whole works — me and Punk [Pauline, who was Bonnie's sister] and Zenobia [John Allen's first wife] *went down to see them off — Hoody* [Bonnie's first husband] *was already gone — Navy too — I don't remember his ship either.*

(Two weeks later) will try to get this in mail — you got my job title wrong. I was welder at N.S. [Naval Station] *ship building. Co. Loved it — women were not allowed on ships. We worked out on the "skid" — we call it platform. Long and no top over your head. In winter we couldn't get on enough clothes to stay warm. Summer that sun was really, really hot. Had to wear coveralls and high top shoes to keep the melting steel off our skin —*

Rosie the Riveter

Bonnie Tate, then married to Ewell S. (Hoody) Tate, had worked during the war at the ship building yard in Wilmington, North Carolina. Her son, Don Tate, described her work: "She worked with a 'fitter' who would move the steel plates into position. Mother would tack-weld them into place. Another welder would follow behind her and complete the weld. Mother was proud of what she did in the shipyard and the fact that she could see the results of her work in the finished product. She said the launching of the ship was a very moving event and all the workers were present at the launch. [These were the Liberty ships.]

"This little mountain girl from Polk County, North Carolina, would just beam with pride when she relived those days and these special events. I am so proud of her and I can't think of anyone I have ever met that had a stronger work ethic," Don said.

Bonnie Ruff Allen with her brother Joe Ruff

After the War

John Allen came home from the Pacific and resumed his work as a plumber and carpenter. He designed and handcrafted many decorative items made from wood, such as wishing wells, small ferris wheels, and merry-go-rounds. John passed away in 1987.

John L. Allen

John Allen home on leave. He stands in front of his mother's mill house in Caroleen, North Carolina.

Charles Terry Craft, U.S. Navy

U.S. Navy Aviation Electrician Charles "Bud" Craft

Charles Terry "Bud" Craft joined the U.S. Navy November 9, 1942, served at the Carrier Aircraft Service Unit in Ford Island Naval Air Station in Hawaii, and was discharged as 3rd Class Petty Officer in 1946.

Bud tells his story: "I was born and raised on a farm in Johnson, Ohio. I graduated from Johnson High School in 1940 and I had a one-year scholarship to Ohio State. I planted five acres of potatoes to pay for my next year's college. The blight hit my potatoes and they all died. I didn't have enough money to go back to school, so I went to work at the steel mill, Youngstown Sheet and Tube.

Joining Up after Pearl Harbor

"I was working there when World War II started. On my eighteenth birthday, I got a greeting from Uncle Sam: 'You're going to be drafted.' The next day I went down and enlisted in the Navy. I didn't join the Army because I didn't want to walk. I figured I could sail if I was in the Navy. I joined in Youngstown, Ohio, and they sent me to Cleveland, then Great Lakes for boot training. It was wintertime. Really cold up there. After that, they sent me to Detroit to General Service Electrical School. From there, to Chicago to Aviation Electrician School, then to Alameda Naval Air Station in California."

Bud Craft

242

Preparing for War in the Pacific

"I was there for several months, then got orders to transfer to receiving ship 28, the Healy, in Honolulu. I went over on a passenger ship. The Healy was a destroyer on its shakedown cruise. So I got to go through all their initiation, I guess you'd call it. We had target practice and everything else. It was really quite an interesting trip.

"I had to ride an ammunition train from Honolulu up to the ammunition depot in Lualualei. They had a narrow-gauge railway there with little flatcars on it. Everyone of those had a 500-pound bomb on it. I had to ride up to the ammunition depot with a rifle, straddling one of those bombs. I don't know what defense I could have done with just a rifle.

"We were a storage place for the bombs and all the equipment planning for the invasion of Japan. The battleships came to Pearl Harbor and loaded up. Pearl Harbor was one of the main distributing places. The United States had a surplus of everything. Other countries didn't. I think that's one thing that helped us win the war—the fact that we had warehouses full of stuff in Hawaii, in reserve. It was a nice base. I had a nice cement barracks with terrazzo floors. We had nice ship service and a movie theatre, really a nice base. Some of my buddies were living in tents up on Red Hill. One Seabee schoolmate was living in a Quonset hut."

Ford Island Naval Air Station

"I did that for a while and then they said, 'Get packed up, you're going to be transferred.' So I got everything packed up, went down and threw it on a tugboat. They took me across the harbor to Ford Island Naval Air Station and dumped me off there. There I worked in that big assembly and repair station. It was two chiefs and me and we had a secretary. They sent all their stuff in there for repairs. Ford Island (pictured below) was right in the middle of Pearl Harbor. *The Arizona* [battleship] was right down at the end of Ford Island."

Ford Island—in the middle of Pearl Harbor

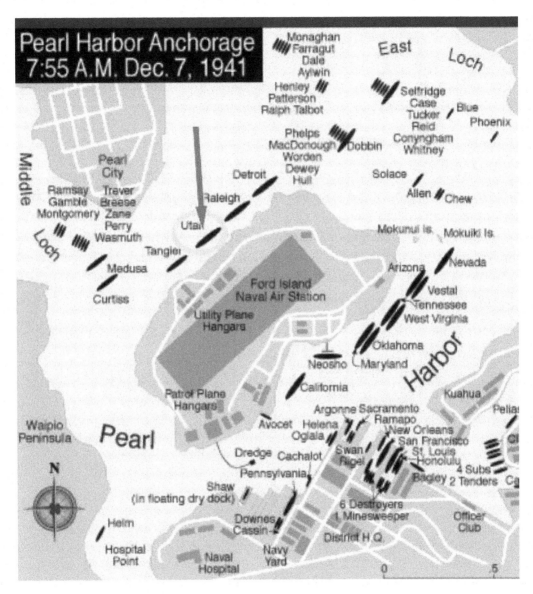

"They were having clean-up in Pearl Harbor after the attack. They raised *The Utah* (see anchorage above) while I was there. I watched it. In Assembly and Repair, we had 30 civilians who volunteered to go over there when the war started. They were all experienced in repairing electrical equipment. I checked in stuff and issued it to somebody to fix it. When they needed spare parts, I had a bicycle and I went over to the salvage yard and get the parts.

"I was at Ford Island for probably eight months. I asked to test for officer candidate school. So they sent me from Honolulu to Asbury Park, New Jersey, for shipping school. They wanted to know what I wanted to take in college. I said, 'Well, I guess I would take electrical engineering.' So they sent me to the University of Illinois. I was there for eight months and I washed out. I couldn't make the grades. It was tough."

Back in the States for Commando Training

"They transferred me back to Alameda Naval Air Station [California] and put me in a commando outfit. I went through intensive commando training. They issued me all the jungle greens and a rifle. In training, we had to run the commando course every day. We had to jump off a scaffold the height of a carrier into the water. We had to take our pants off and tie the legs up with a knot to make life savers out of them. We had rifle practice every day. They put boxing gloves on you and made you fight some guy. They always put me with this left-handed guy, and he hit me in the nose because I was guarding from the wrong side.

"My older sister, Dorothy, was an officer in the WAVES in San Francisco when I was at Alameda. Every time I saw her, I had to salute her because she had a higher rank than I did. She went to New Orleans and was in charge of keeping track of where every service man was—she was keeping records."

Bud's father, Bud, sister Dorothy in WAVES uniform, and Bud's mother

After the War Ends

"I was all set to go, but two days before we were leaving the states, they said they had too many electrician mates and transferred me to back into CASU (Carrier Aircraft Service Unit) again. By this time, the war was over. Every morning they had me stay in the barracks and every morning I had to report with my gear. They said, 'You're going to transfer.' But every morning they'd call my name and say, 'Craft, you're scratched. You've got too many points.' Points meant you're getting ready for discharge.

"I did this for about a week. One morning, they said, 'Craft, you're going home.' So they sent me home to Toledo, Ohio. That was 1946. I ran into Bill Porter, a buddy of mine, who was home for a 10-day leave. He said, 'Let's just re-enlist. There's nothing left here. The girls are all gone.' I said, 'Well, let me go home and look anyway.' The first night I was home, Bill had a car and said, 'Let's go out on the town. I've got a date with girl over in Kinsman. We'll see if we can find you a date.' Kinsman was the next town.

"So we went over to Kinsman to get this girl. We were sitting there in Bill's car waiting for her to come out of her house. This other car pulled up next to us with a girl in it. Bill got to talking with her and he said, 'We're going bowling, would you like to go with us?' She said, 'Sure.' So she jumped in the back seat with me. We sat there and waited and waited and Bill's girl never came out. We found out later that she went out the back door of the house. So Bill was there with no date and I had a date. Then another car pulled up. My date, Shirley, knew this girl, and talked her into going bowling with us. Shirley became my wife.

Bud and Shirley Craft

"So I went back and went to work in the Youngstown Sheet and Tube mill in Youngstown, Ohio. The first thing they did was go on strike. That disgusted me and so I left there and got a job at Westinghouse in Sharon, Pennsylvania, working as an electrician. A buddy of mine talked me into going back to school. He said, 'Why don't you become an industrial arts teacher?' Well, I didn't even know what industrial arts was. So I went to Kent State on the G.I. Bill. Then graduated from Ohio State and taught high school industrial arts for 30 years. I enjoyed that. I had always liked carpentry work."

Family

"My wife, Shirley June, and I had four children—a girl, Julie and three boys: Tom, Chris, and Kelly. Shirley and I were married for 69 years. Sadly, she passed away. My three boys all put four years in the Navy. I'm very proud of all my children."

Above: Shirley, Chris, Bud, and Bud's mother, Grandma Ella Craft

Below, from left, sons Chris, Tom, and Kelly. All served in the U.S. Navy.

Bud's and Shirley's 50th wedding anniversary

Front row, from left, daughter Julie, Bud, Shirley, and the pastor who married Bud and
Shirley 50 years earlier. Back row, sons Kelly, Chris, and Tom

Bud continues, "I built a chalet up in Sapphire, North Carolina—built it all myself. I wired it, I plumbed it—I could do all that stuff. That house burned and I had to re-build. Now I live in Florida in the winter and in Sapphire in the summer, where my daughter and son live. I have six grandchildren and six great-grandchildren."

Family reunion at the chalet Bud built in Sapphire, N.C.

Below, Bud at home and with his beagles

Asked what he would like to tell young people, Bud said, "I think it should be mandatory for every young person to spend at least two years in service. I think it would give them discipline. My boys all put that four years in and I think it did them good. They all seemed to learn a lot in there and came out with good experience."

Darrell Watson, U.S. Marines

Second Lieutenant Darrell Watson, Active Marine Corps Reserves, 1943

*Darrell Watson enlisted in the U.S. Marines
in 1942, at age 20, and served in the Active Marine Corps Reserves until 1946.*

Headed to the Pacific

Twenty-year-old Darrell Watson from Chincoteague, Virginia, volunteered for the U.S. Marines. He tells his story. "When the war started, I was a student at The College of William and Mary, majoring in business and government administration. I graduated on June 9, 1942. On June 12, I was in a Marine recruiting office. My service began in Quantico, Virginia, where I entered Officer Candidate School. I became a Second Lieutenant. I later did a year's duty in Scotia, N.Y., at the Naval Supply Depot.

"I asked for a transfer to go overseas, went to Camp LeJeune, N.C. for additional training, and was assigned to a replacement battalion to go to the Pacific in 1944.

"We went to Pavuvu in the Solomon Islands, where I was assigned to an engineering regiment as Assistant Adjutant, in charge of all the records of the battalion. Later I was promoted to Battalion Adjutant while preparing for the movement of our division to the Okinawa campaign.

"We had 5,000 replacement troops assigned to our battalion going into Okinawa. We landed there April 1, 1945, which was Easter Sunday. We were responsible for unloading supplies on the beach until the Army and the Navy port battalions took over, relieving us, to set up stockpiles for the campaign. This was everything the troops needed: food, arms, tractors, supplies, and other equipment. We were replacing the killed and wounded. I also sent, when requested, the personnel with the qualifications needed—riflemen, medical personnel, artillery, etc.

"The battle in Okinawa was nearly over. I was sent to set up a headquarters on Okinawa to prepare for the invasion of Japan.

"My closest call came when our battalion was bombed on the beach, but I had gone to another beach to straighten out the working party. A Japanese plane came over, strafing, dropping bombs on the beach. I jumped out of my jeep and got behind a rock, so I wasn't hit.

"I drove back to the command post and found my Sergeant Major lying on the ground. He was badly injured. But God was looking after me that day. If I had not taken that little assignment to the other beach, about a mile away, I'd be lying there too.

Second Lieutenant Darrell Watson on Okinawa, Japan in 1945 (in happier times)

256

"When we heard they had dropped the atomic bomb, we were all happy that the combat was over. In October, 1945, we were sent to Tientsin, China, to disarm the Japanese troops. We lived in quarters that the Japanese had taken over; we were lodged in a British-American Tobacco Company warehouse."

Career After the War

"In January, 1946, we came back to San Francisco and then to Norfolk, where I was separated from active duty in April. I stayed in the reserves as a Major until 1958.

"I went to Ormond Beach, Florida to see my fiancé, Mary Irene, whom I later married in October, 1946. I went to work for Dun & Bradstreet as business reporter and manager in the U.S. and Canada, and stayed with them for 25 years. Mary Irene and I moved to Georgia, where I became credit manager for two different steel distribution companies. We moved to Hendersonville in 2012. Mary Irene passed away in 2013.

"I was not a hero; I was strictly an administrative officer. I had one injury during the war— a broken hand while playing baseball against an Army team." Darrell smiled, "We won the game."

Darrell Watson in 2016

Edwin Holcombe, U.S. Navy

Aviation Machinist Mate 2nd Class Ed Holcombe

*Ed Holcombe entered the U.S. Navy in 1942 and
served until 1946.*

In the Navy

Ed tells the story of his service in World War II. "I was born in Ball Ground, Georgia. I graduated from North Georgia College in 1941 and went to work in Columbia, S.C., with an industrial supply company. I went to Atlanta to join the Army Air Corps. I was accepted, but couldn't pass the vision exam. I tried to join the Navy, but their vision requirement also stopped me. Then in August, 1942, I got a letter from the Navy that they had lowered their vision requirements and invited me to re-apply. I immediately quit my job and joined the Navy.

"I went to boot camp in Pensacola, Florida. Boot camp was usually called 'hell month,' but it turned out to be a good experience for me. The guy in charge of drilling quickly discovered that I would do a better job of drilling than he did, so he made me the drill sergeant. Most of the guys would ask me to let them fall in on the quadrangle and practice after the evening meal, so they got pretty good.

"I had an easy job—just sitting up there on the porch and drilling them. I had it easy. No mess cooking, no apartment cleaning, no anything. I had it the best in the world," Ed smiled. "And I won the Last Day Parade in drilling. We came in first out of twelve."

Pensacola to Pearl Harbor

"I went to work as an air traffic controller in the control tower at Pensacola. I was promoted to Aviation Machinist Mate Second Class, and turned down offers to attend Navy Officer School because I wanted to get my pilot's wings. I was selected for Aviation Cadet Flight Training in California, but again the vision test prevented me from flying.

"When I was sent to Pearl Harbor in '43, I became head of the aircraft engine overhaul shop. We were the airfield and stop for aircraft flying to the Pacific Islands. When the atomic bombs were dropped, there was jubilation. The war was over and we were going home. I came home and was discharged in 1946."

Aviation Machinist Mate 2nd Class Ed Holcombe on Pearl Harbor

Life After the War

"I came back to Charleston Supply Company in South Carolina as a warehouse superintendent and later manager. I stayed with them for 44 years. I married Leila and we moved to Hendersonville four years ago. Last August we celebrated our 70th wedding anniversary."

Ed recalled, "In my spare time, I was a judge for the Scottish Highland Games at Grandfather Mountain, N.C., serving as Director of Highland Athletics there and at Charleston, S.C., for many years."

Ed Holcombe (on the left) judges the caber toss at Charleston, South Carolina's Highland Games.

Ed Holcombe (on the left) with actor Charlton Heston (right) in Central Park, N.Y., in 1983. Heston was given the caber to attempt a toss. When he dropped it he said, "I guess I'm better at driving chariots," referring to his role in the movie *Ben-hur.*

Ed Holcombe in 2016

Paul Eric Spencer, U.S. Navy

Retired Captain Paul Spencer, U.S. Navy, 1968

Paul Spencer joined the U.S. Navy in California in 1942 and served until 1968.

Pilot Training

Eighteen-year-old Paul Spencer signed up for the Navy Reserves Aviation Cadet Program on December 2, 1942, a year after the Japanese attack on Pearl Harbor.

Paul tells his story. "Interestingly, President George H.W. Bush signed up on his 18th birthday, June 12 of '42, so he beat me to the starting point of getting trained. He breezed through the training in nine months. I identify with George Bush because I was just a little behind him in time. He was shot down near a Japanese-held island and luckily was picked up by an American submarine. Several other pilots shot down that day in the same vicinity were picked up by the Japanese, held as prisoners of war, and treated very severely.

"By the time I joined six months later than George Bush started, I faced a backlog, so I had to sit home and wait to start my education as a naval aviator. The wait turned out to be over six months.

"In June of 1943, the Navy sent me to the University of Texas, in Austin. We'd walk around with a wooden rifle in the quadrangle and pretend like we were being trained. No airplanes! We were just going to ordinary classes. Then a group of us were sent to Kerrville, Texas where we learned to fly Piper Cubs, just a civilian airplane. With many more delays and training on other bases, I finally got my wings on January 10, 1945. I was assigned as a fighter pilot and sent to Daytona Beach, Florida, to learn how to fly the Grumman F6F Hellcat.

"The next step was to learn how to take off and land on an aircraft carrier. The Navy no longer had a carrier in the Gulf of Mexico, where pilots had previously trained. It was now too dangerous because of the presence of German submarines in the Gulf. The Germans could sink anything they saw there. So, the Navy made 'make-do' carriers by converting two former Great Lakes coal carriers. They reconfigured them with flat decks and arresting gear and made their home port Chicago. They were named *Wolverine* and *Sable*. I successfully made my required 14 landings and take-offs on the *Sable* on Lake Michigan.

Asked what it was like the first time he landed, Paul said, "It was just plain fun. When the sun is shining, the wind is not blowing, and the seas are calm, it's like the best amusement park ride you'd like to be on. It's just wonderful!"

Victory in Japan

"When VJ Day was declared, I was stationed in Oakland, California, waiting for my assigned squadron to show up. On that day I went to San Francisco and watched sailors and the crowds celebrating. Some were trying to overturn cable cars. You can't turn over a cable car, it's impossible. But they were trying. They could only rock them back and forth. Everybody was going crazy over our victory in Japan."

Fighter Pilot

"A few days later Fighter Squadron 17 (that I was waiting for) arrived in San Francisco fresh from fighting the war in the Pacific flying F4U Corsairs. I joined them. The war was over and peacetime activity for the Navy was the order of the day. The squadron was then moved to the Naval Air Station, Fallon, Nevada.

"While at NAS Fallon a wonderful opportunity for change in my military status was offered by the Navy. They offered a transfer from US Navy Reserve to the Regulars of the Navy. In return each officer would receive college tuition with full pay to bring us up to five semesters total and a nine-month course at the Navy War College to bring us up to the standard of the education of a Naval Academy graduate. I immediately accepted this life-changing opportunity.

"Fighter Squadron 17 then moved to NAS Brunswick, Maine, followed by NAS Oceana, Virginia. Then I left the squadron with orders to proceed to Washington, D.C. and to George Washington University for three semesters of college.

"After George Washington University I was assigned to Fighter Squadron 23 at NAS Oceana, Virginia. The squadron, flying F4U Corsairs, completed a six month deployment to the Mediterranean aboard the carrier *Coral Sea*.

"I was then assigned to the Naval War College in Newport, Rhode Island, for the junior curriculum. Within a month the war in Korea broke out. The course was canceled and I was assigned to the Training Command in Pensacola, Florida and was a flight instructor for two years.

"My next assignment was to go to a Navy school to learn the skills of being a member of the Combat Information Center on a Navy Aircraft Carrier, with a following assignment to the USS Naval Carrier *Yorktown*. I completed the training course and joined the *Yorktown* in Alameda, California. I spent 20 months on the carrier, mostly in the Pacific Ocean.

"Next it was back to the main business of being a fighter pilot. I was assigned to Fighter Squadron VF-153 at Moffat Field, Mountain View, California, flying North American Aircraft Company FJ-3s and subsequently Grumman F9F-8s. We had a Western Pacific cruise.

"Then along came the other special treatment given me for integrating into the Regular Navy. I was assigned to the Navy Postgraduate School in Monterey, California, for nine months. The purpose was to add the military subjects that a Naval Academy graduate is exposed to."

Naval Test Pilot

"I received orders at the end of my study at Monterey to attend the Navy Test Pilot School at Patuxent River Naval Air Station in Patuxent. Maryland. This school is one of the most important duty assignments a Naval Aviator can hope for. It's very selective and a feather in your hat. In my class I studied with three astronauts-to-be. They were Wally Schirra, Jim Lovell and Pete Conrad. All three of them subsequently went to the moon and back.

Photo above:

Pete Conrad, front row, far right:, was on Apollo 12, the second module to land on the moon.
Wally Shirra, third row, far left, was one of the first 7 astronauts to ride a rocket into space.
Jim Lovell, third row, 3rd from the right, became commander of Apollo 13.
Paul Spencer, back row, 3rd from the right, became Commander of a fighter squadron of F-4s.

"Following the school I was assigned to the Carrier Suitability Division of Test Flight. At that time I became the lead test pilot for testing the F-4 Phantom's suitability to operate from our aircraft carriers. The plane (pictured at right) was the heaviest fighter the Navy had up to that point. Its two engines had a total of 34,000 pounds of thrust and weighed 34,000 pounds, empty of fuel and munitions. After we exhaustively

completed tests leading up to flying off a Navy carrier, we flew it to the Norfolk, Virginia Naval Air Station and had the plane hoisted aboard the *USS Independence*. We put to sea on a Monday and started testing in the real environment. Everything went fine with all of our tests until Friday when we had a failure of the tailhook.

"When I came in for a landing that day I caught the arresting gear cable and began to come to a stop. The normal stopping distance for an arrested landing is 300 feet, but at approximately 150 feet of runout the tailhook came apart very near the attachment point of the airplane. The broken part of the tailhook stopped and I was immediately in a very slow airplane.

"Upon touching the deck on a carrier landing the pilot is required to apply full power, less the afterburner. Immediately after I sensed my predicament, I applied both afterburners. I dropped off the deck with not enough airspeed to maintain altitude. As I neared the surface of the sea I had gained just enough airspeed to avoid touching the water. I flew away, landed at a nearby Marine Airbase, refueled, and flew back to NAS Patuxent River.

Retired Navy Captain Paul Spencer holding the broken tail hook piece from his memorable test of the F-4 Phantom (The chrome-plated tail hook rests on his hearth.)

"The manufacturer of the plane redesigned the tailhook and future tests were successful. They graciously chrome-plated the intact part of the broken tailhook and presented it to me.

"Subsequently, as a test pilot, I was the only pilot to ever fly an F-4 Phantom on a night carrier landing on the *U.S.S. Intrepid,* which is now a museum in New York City Harbor. My professional recommendation to my seniors was to not assign any fighter squadron flying F-4s to any Intrepid class carrier. The length of the flight deck landing area was marginal compared to the more modern carriers such as the *Forrestal.*"

First Command

"My tour at Patuxent and my assignment as test pilot for the F-4 Phantom resulted in selection as Executive Officer of VF-74, the first Navy Fighter Squadron to fly the Phantom. The squadron was part of Air Wing Eight based at NAS Virginia Beach,

Virginia. After a year as Executive Officer I was moved up to Commanding Officer. I had a successful deployment on the *USS Forr*estal to the Mediterranean.

"My next assignment was to the Navy War College Senior Course in Newport, Rhode Island. After War College I got the pinnacle Navy flying command—an Air Wing. It was Air Wing Eight on the *USS Forrestal*. I joined the *Forrestal* in the middle of a deployment in the Mediterranean and took command of the Air Wing. I left the *Forrestal* in the middle of its next deployment to the Med. All this time the war in Vietnam was raging on the other half of the world!"

The Pentagon

"As I left the *Forrestal* I was promoted to Captain. I spent my last three years in the Navy at the Pentagon, assigned to the Office of the Chief of Naval Operations. The Pentagon has a great many admirals and generals, so being captain is not a big deal. The Vietnam War raged on."

A Decision

"After the Pentagon I envisioned that to stay in the Navy, I must make myself eligible for promotion to Rear Admiral. At this career stage a Navy pilot must make a major change from flying airplanes to commanding ships and forces. My next assignment would have to be a successful command of a large, deep draft Navy ship. After that I would need to be selected and have a successful command of an aircraft carrier. Then my name would appear on a list to be selected to Rear Admiral and sent to a Navy selection board. When the board came to the name of Paul Spencer they would find no combat experience in his career. I would probably be rejected. I took a 30-day leave and tried my luck at getting a job flying. Surprisingly I was successful."

American Express Company

"I got a job with American Express. I was the first pilot they ever had. Overnight I was the corporate aviation expert! They had already purchased a plane, a beautiful French-made eight passenger twin jet. I hired a co-pilot and a mechanic. I rented hangar, shop, and office space and began flying their executives to destinations of their choice. Over the 16 years I was with them, we grew to five jet airplanes and one helicopter."

Retirement

"I retired from American Express at age 60. My wife Judy worked full time in her tour operator's business in our home in Stamford, Connecticut. I joined her business and helped Judy and her three workers to be successful. In 1995 we moved ourselves and the business to Brevard, North Carolina, where we are now. In 2015 we dissolved the business."

Paul and Judy Spencer in 2016

James Brush, U.S. Army

SP4 James Brush, U.S. Army

James Brush joined the U.S. Army in 1943. He worked on the Manhattan District Project in Los Alamos to develop the atom bomb, and later worked at the Navy Sea Systems Command in Washington, D.C., as an engineer and supervisor.

James Brush was born in Washington, D.C. on November 21, 1924. He graduated from Bethesda-Chevy Chase High School in 1942 and entered Massachusetts Institute of Technology. He had completed one semester when he was called to active duty in March of 1943. After basic training, he was sent to the Citadel in Charleston, S.C., for classification purposes. This resulted in his attending a year and a half of engineering courses at Rutgers University (Army Specialized Training Program).

Jim was stationed at Los Alamos, New Mexico, from January of 1945 through February of 1946. He worked on the Manhattan District Project to develop the atom bomb to end World War II.

His assignments included construction of test equipment, firefighting details, and guard duty at the Trinity site during the test of the bomb (in the event of fallout dangers to nearby sheep ranchers). During the night, in preparation for detonation of the bomb, Jim was instructed to lie down and shield his eyes. Early the next day, he was aware of a blinding light followed shortly by a thunderous roar. They were without protection because they were a few miles away in the desert.

After each three-month period, the top achievers were retained and the rest were sent as "casual replacements", going directly to the front, as in D-Day. Out of 300 students, Jim was one of the very few left, and was sent to Los Alamos for the rest of the war.

Returning to M.I.T. after the war, and using the G.I. Bill, Jim completed his degree in Electronics Engineering in 1948. He worked for the Navy Sea Systems Command in Washington, D.C. as an engineer and supervisor, managing programs that provided electronic equipment for our ships.

Jim was married to Penny and they had three children. Penny passed away after the children were grown. Jim and his second wife, Evie (married in 1980) have a daughter who was born in 1984, when they also retired to live in Mills River, N.C.

Genealogy is one of Jim's hobbies, and helping other people put together their applications to patriot organizations. He is the registrar of the local Sons of the American Revolution Chapter and is treasurer of the Western Colony Mayflower Society. Jim and Evie are active, founding members of the Holy Family Episcopal Church in Mills River, N.C.

When Jim was interviewed by his stepdaughter for a college paper, she asked him, "What did it feel like to be eighteen, an only son, and the whole world was at war?" He responded that he saw it as his patriotic duty to sign up with the Army and go into active service for his country, without a second thought. His wife, Evie, adds, "God spared him. He is now in his mid-nineties and in a wheelchair, but in good health." Jim has ten grandchildren and three great-grandchildren.

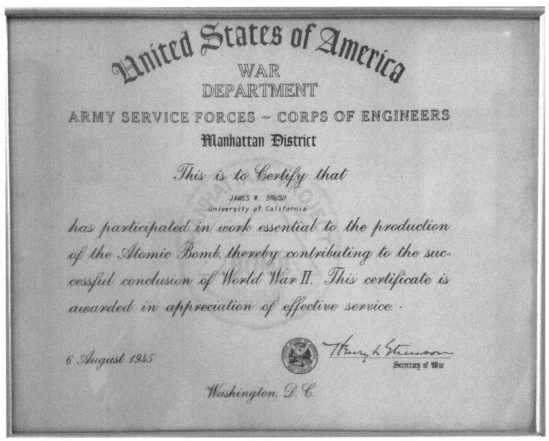

James Brush's certificate from the War Department: "This is to certify that James W. Brush, University of California, has participated in work essential to the production of the Atomic Bomb, thereby contributing to the successful conclusion of World War II. This certificate is awarded in appreciation of effective service."

Signed by Secretary of War Henry L. Stimson on August 5, 1945

**James Brush's uniform with Atomic Patch U.S. Army, WWII
Special Engineer Detachment, Los Alamos, New Mexico**

The uniform and photos shown in this story are displayed in the Veterans History Museum of the Carolinas in Brevard, N.C., generously provided by James and Evelyn Brush. James Brush's story was written by his wife, Evelyn Brush.

Mitchell Kostro, U.S. Army

Corporal Mitchell Kostro, U.S. Army

Mitchell Kostro served as Gunner Tank 2736in the 96th Infantry, 763rd Tank Battalion in the Pacific. He was drafted on May 1, 1943 and was discharged January 18, 1946.

Mitch Kostro's story: "I was born in Chicago and graduated from Chicago High School in 1942. I attended the University of Illinois in Champagne, where I spent one year. During that time, I was drafted into the Army. I went to Camp McCoy for basic training. Then I went to Fort Sill, Oklahoma, then to Fort Ord, California. I was in the tank battalion in Hawaii. We were replacing the federalized National Guard that was assigned to Maui to get ready for combat in the Pacific. We were moving toward the eventual invasion of Japan.

"I got pneumonia and was hospitalized in Hawaii, and later sent to the Philippines. I was a gunner in a tank. We had five soldiers assigned to a tank. There we made an amphibious landing in Leyte, in the Philippines. For this I received a bronze arrowhead (shown at center of ribbon at bottom in the photo below) on my ribbons to signify this beachhead landing.

"Mitch remembers once, all the tanks were parked on the beach. When the tide came in, it covered the tanks with seawater, which ruined them."

Corporal Mitch Kostro

"The Japanese soldiers fought in caves in the mountains. A lot of the Japanese soldiers were killed in the caves. The Japanese Army removed their bodies, but they left their weapons.

"I found a Japanese soldier's rifle in a cave and brought it home." Mitch donated that rifle, pictured below, to the Veterans History Museum of the Carolinas in Brevard, N.C.

Below, this Japanese soldier's rifle is displayed in the museum's
World War II – Pacific Gallery.

Mitch Kostro

Mitch donated his uniform jacket to the Veterans History Museum of the Carolinas. Pictured below are the jacket and some of his patches.

Mitch's medals listed on his discharge are:

- Bronze arrowhead (signifying amphibious landing at Leyte)

- Good conduct (Mitch joked, "Which isn't very much.")

- Southern Philippines

- Okinawa

- Asiatic-Pacific Service

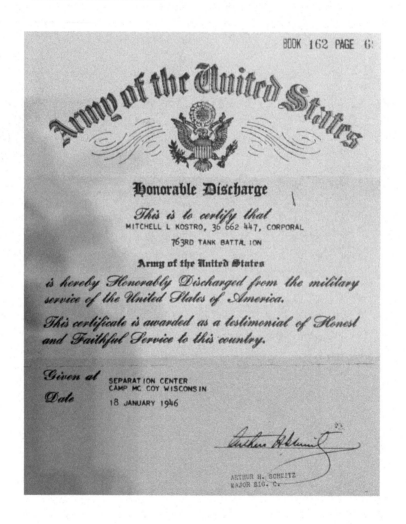

After the War

After the war, Mitch taught social studies and history at Crane High School in Chicago. That's where he met his wife, Dorothy, who was a math teacher at the same school. We went as teacher chaperones to that high school's prom, so we "went to the prom together" and were married in 1956. Mitch earned his Master's degree from University of Illinois in Champagne and did post-graduate work at Navy Pier in Chicago.

They have one son, Charles, who lives in Urbana, Illinois. Dorothy and Mitch moved to Hendersonville, N.C. when they retired, loving the outdoors and camping. They have traveled to 124 countries and all seven continents, including Antarctica's South Pole. Mitch and Dorothy went to the Philippines and met the family of someone Mitch knew when he was stationed there.

Mitch and Dorothy Kostro in their home in Columbus, N.C. in 2019

Robert C. "Bob" Frank, U.S. Navy

Seaman Robert C. Frank, when he entered the U.S. Navy in 1943

*Bob Frank, born in 1924 in Rochester, New York, was drafted into the U.S. Navy
in March, 1943, and served until April 1946.
He was discharged in 1964 as Storekeeper (D) First Class.*

In the Navy: Training and Preparation

In 1943, nineteen-year-old Bob Frank began his boot camp training in the U.S. Navy at Sampson Naval Training Center in the Finger Lakes area near Rochester, New York. He tells his story: "At Sampson, I remember 20 of us fellas got off a bus, took off our civilian clothes, and put on our Navy issue to start our training. The man in charge asked, 'Who can type?' I raised my hand. I was the only one who said I could type. You know, I was just a farm kid. I don't know why I took typing, but I took typing. I had no other basic skills, but I could type as well as a lot of the girls in class. So I just have to say that during my time, I did more typing than shooting.

285

"So they made me Storekeeper, in charge of payroll. Storekeeper sounds like a bit of a misnomer for my job—I didn't keep supplies. I think Storekeeper just meant anyone who worked with numbers and could type. I was a very popular guy once a month when I figured the pay and paid them off in cash. It kept up the morale. It was a nice job," Bob laughed.

"At Sampson, when we were high enough up in a building, we could see cargo ships and battleships going up and down in the Atlantic Ocean. We knew there were German submarines all along the Atlantic coast.

"So of course I thought I'd be deployed to the Atlantic when I finished my training—I could see the ships! But instead of sending me just 300 miles to the Atlantic, they sent me 3,000 miles to Bremerton, Washington, near Seattle. I got orders to go to the Aleutian Islands in Alaska. My buddies said, 'Oh, you'll love it up there. There's a woman behind every tree.' And don't forget, I was 19 years old. I couldn't wait to get up to the Aleutian Islands. I was up there for several months," he laughed, "but I never saw a tree."

Preparing for the Invasion of Japan

"I joined PT (patrol torpedo) Squadron 13 in Alaska. We returned to San Francisco to prepare for the invasion of Japan. We put new guns, torpedoes, and depth chargers on boats. When the boats were ready for action, we put four of those PT boats on the deck of a Liberty Ship, chained them down, and the Liberty Ship went to the South Pacific. We stopped in New Guinea and took the PT boats off the Liberty Ship. Then the PT boats went under their own power to Borneo. My career was with PTs. We were Squadron 13 and we traveled with Squadron 16—two squadrons of PT boats. We didn't see a lot of action. This was 1944 and the Japs had been chased out, pretty much. Still a few battles, but not much. Once I found a sea bag left behind by one of the Japanese. Inside it was a rising sun flag with a lot of names written on it. I later donated it to the military museum that was built where I had taken my basic training.

"As a Storekeeper, I didn't have to ride the boats, so I didn't have to go where the shooting was very often. I was on the base, working a calculator and typing, more than I was fighting. We were on bases in Borneo, New Guinea, and the Philippines.

"I was brought up in the '30s, so I was not a beer drinker. My father had died in 1930 when I was six. It was just my mother and me during the Depression, so there was no money for anything like beer. I was an only child, so it was harder on my mother, probably, seeing me go off to war, than it was on me.

"But every month, every sailor was issued two cans of beer and told, 'You can go to another island and just relax.' You know, a recreation type thing. I didn't want the beer, so I used my two cans like cash. I used them to buy paint from the painting locker. I used it to paint my boxes—boxes that I packed my typewriter and calculator in when we moved to a new port. You do things sometimes just to keep busy. I still don't drink beer," he chuckled.

"We went into Borneo. Then we went to take the Philippines, on the island of Mindoro. I was on an LST (landing ship, tank) that had pulled up on the shore. The doors were open. Everyone else was hauling parts out, but for some reason, I stayed in the LST. All of a sudden, a Japanese suicide plane flew over the land, looked back, and apparently saw our LST with the doors open. He circled back. I guess he thought, 'I can blow that ship all to pieces when I go down.' I watched him coming toward me. The gunners on the deck had 20 or 40 millimeter guns and they were shooting at him. They must have hit him. Just before he got to the doors of our ship, he crashed on the land.

"I had already seen several suicide bombers crashing into LSTs. Sometimes the LSTs that had been hit came on into port, and we went on board to see if we could save somebody. I saw dead bodies blown to the ceiling and still hanging there. This could have happened to me. My life was saved. I have to believe that somebody up there was watching.

"Camped on one of the islands one night, I was asleep on my cot. I woke up hearing Japanese bombers that kept getting closer and closer, so I rolled off my cot onto the floor as the bombs went off. The next morning I counted 52 holes in my tent from shrapnel. If I had stood up, I probably would've been hit."

Back in the States when the War Ended

"I was sent to Boston and discharged in April of '46 as Storekeeper First Class. Three chevrons on my sleeve. While I was overseas I had moved up from Storekeeper Third Class. On the G.I. Bill, I graduated from the University of Rochester in 1950. In September that year, I went to work for Rochester Gas & Electric. I was a personnel manager who went around to the colleges and recruited and hired engineers. I retired after 35 years.

"I have two battle ribbons (among others) that I can identify—the Good Conduct Ribbon and the Philippine Liberation Ribbon. The South Pacific was a beautiful place. White beaches, swaying palm trees, Japanese suicide bombers in the sky," Bob quipped with a smile.

"After retirement we moved to Seneca Lake, N.Y., near Sampson Naval Training Center where I had started." Then after living in Florida and Grandfather Mountain, N.C., Bob and his wife Marlene moved to Brevard in 2001.

Marlene and Bob Frank
in 2016

William "Bill" Siniard, U.S. Navy

William Siniard, Seaman Second Class, U.S. Navy, 1943

William "Bill" Siniard joined the U.S. Navy in 1943 when he was 17 years old.
He served in Europe and in the Pacific until being discharged in 1947.

A Young Man in Brevard

Bill Siniard tells his story. "My daddy ran a trucking company in Brevard, N.C. He delivered loads of wood, loads of stone, and moved furniture for people. One time he sent me to Canton, N.C. to get a family's furniture and move them to Brevard. In that family was a 10-year-old girl named Frances. I didn't pay her no never-mind. More about her later."

In the Navy on Merchant Ships Traveling to Europe

"I volunteered for the U.S. Navy when I was 17 years old. My parents signed for me to join. I went to Bainbridge, Maryland, for basic training and then to Brooklyn, New York, to the Armed Guards Center. Then to North Carolina, where

I got on a merchant ship, the *S.S. John Hathorn* (a civilian ship), carrying a big load of tobacco headed to Europe. U.S. Navy personnel were assigned as gunners (armed guards) to travel on merchant ships with escorts (convoys), to defend the merchant ships against German submarines. I made five trips to Europe.

"Every once in a while we'd see a sub get blown up. We had patrol crafts alongside that would drop depth charges to locate the submarines. The submarines had been shot by the U.S. Navy destroyers and destroyer escorts. We had the guns in case we could see them, but they were underwater so we couldn't see the submarines. We operated the guns if we had to defend the merchant ship. When we got to Europe or Africa, we'd use the guns to protect that ship. The last trip I made was going up the St. George's Channel between Ireland and England. It was torpedoed one afternoon about 5:30. The ship sank and we were in the water. We had life boats and life jackets. Some of us got picked up that afternoon, some that night, and some the next day.

"I went on the merchant ships through the Suez Canal and down the Tigris-Euphrates River in Italy. We had tanks and planes and food and tobacco and supplies. We were taking supplies to our troops.

"Once while I was stationed in Brooklyn I was given a 17-day leave for R&R. They sent groups of people to Deland, Florida, for R&R. I told them I wanted to go home to North Carolina to help my family plant the spring crops on the family farm. They said, 'OK' So that's what I did. We didn't really have a farm," he laughed, "but we had a few rows of corn, beans, potatoes, squash, tomatoes and cucumbers. I exaggerated a little.

In photo at left, Bill Siniard is shown at right with his double-first cousin Charlie Siniard, home on leave.

290

"My brother came to Brooklyn looking for me and couldn't find me. They told him I was on a 'Farm Leave.' He said to the officer, 'When in the hell did we get a farm?' So when I went back to Brooklyn, they had a record of it all. They knew then that my family didn't have a farm. The officer said, 'I think we'll take an anchor and tie it around your neck and throw you in the Atlantic Ocean. Get your butt out of here!'"

In the Pacific

"After the war ended in Europe I came back to the States and they shipped 500 of us out to San Diego on a troop train. There they put us on different ships and we went to the Philippines, and then to Okinawa. I was in Okinawa when the war ended, and I got to see one of my brothers there. He was on a Yard Minesweeper-176, there for the invasion of Okinawa. There were four of us brothers in the Navy. There were 17 in all from my family including my cousins. We were all in the Navy except for one who was a paratrooper who jumped into the Philippines and broke his leg.

"In Okinawa I was in a tent city. Every morning they posted a schedule, so we went to see what we were assigned to do. One morning I looked at the schedule and saw my brother's name. That's when I found out he was right there in Okinawa. I went up there and saw him. That was really nice.

"My brother Sydney "Dick" Siniard was on a minesweeper. The Japs would put mines in the water close to the shore—in about six to eight feet of water—so our minesweepers pulled a cable to draw the mines up and our guys would shoot the mines and blow them up when they popped up out of the water. Sometimes the Japanese would swim out to the mine sweepers and try to get on board to try to take over the boat. Our guys would shoot their hands with 45-caliber machine guns when they saw them grab onto the gunwale.

"I wasn't in combat in Okinawa. I was a Gunner's Mate, but my ship, the *U.S.S. Anchor,* did repairs on other ships that had been damaged or broke down. We would cast the ship a line and work on the ship. We were like a floating garage.

"I was there when the atomic bombs were dropped that ended the war. If they hadn't done that, we would have lost 200,000 or 300,000 men trying to fight the Japanese. My brothers and I all made it and came back home. The *U.S.S. Anchor* brought me back to San Diego when the war was over.

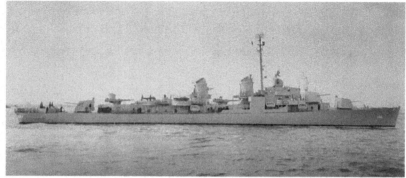

From San Diego, I was on the *U.S.S. Ingraham* (pictured) to Seattle, Washington, where I was discharged. I got an Asiatic-Pacific Ribbon, an American Theatre Ribbon, a World War II Victory Medal, a European-Africa-Middle East Ribbon, and a Good Conduct Ribbon."

After the War

"On January 26, 1947, discharged in Seattle, they paid me six cents a mile to get myself back home. I took a train to Asheville. I went back to driving trucks and also worked with my brother in a garage repairing cars and trucks and tractors.

"Remember that 10-year-old girl, Frances, whose family I moved from Canton before I went in service? Well, after I came home I met her again at the Chatterbox Sandwich Shop on Broad Street in Brevard. She was seven years younger than I was, but we got married.

Bill Siniard, age 18 or 19

292

"While I was fixing cars in the daytime, I ran a projector at a movie theater at night. It was my daddy's drive-in theatre. It was located where the Sagebrush Restaurant is now. Daddy built a large screen and put it up on telephone poles, about 10-12 feet off the ground. It was made of lumber and covered with white asphalt shingles. He set a 16mm projector on a table and showed movies. People didn't have TVs, so they just came and sat down on the ground and watched the movies. Daddy charged a dollar a carload. I ran the projector. Frances sold the popcorn.

"Then I went to work at Ecusta Paper Mill on the clean-up crew. Then I was promoted to the machine room where we made cigarette paper and printing paper. I worked on the set-up and then got to running the machine. We had some of the largest cigarette paper machines in the world. I made supervisor and worked there for 37½ years.

"Everything's worked out pretty good. We have four children and have had a good life."

Bill and Frances Siniard in 2016

Dorothy Managan, U.S. Army

2nd Lt. Dorothy Managan, U.S. Army Nurse

Dorothy Johanna Tonjes Managan joined the U.S. Army as a Nurse in 1945. Head of a ward at Fort Lewis' Madigan Hospital, she took care of POWs returning from the Pacific at the end of WWII. She was discharged in 1946.

"I was born on January 5, 1923, in Flushing, New York, and grew up there. World War II was going on in Europe when I was in high school. I graduated in 1941 and went into the three-year hospital program for nursing, to get my R.N. at the Medical College of Virginia

School of Nursing in Richmond. I decided that I was going into the Army when I finished nursing school—they were asking for nurses. My father, a carpenter by trade, had served in the Army during WWI in Europe. West Point was nearby, just up the Hudson River, and we had gone there. So the Army seemed like the way to go for me.

We're at War

"I was shocked and dismayed when I heard about the attack on Pearl Harbor on the radio.

"Frances Payne Bolton, the Congresswoman from Cleveland, Ohio, got a bill passed through Congress to create the Cadet Nurse Corps. The nursing school at Western Reserve University was named after her. My senior year in nursing, I was part of the Cadet Nurse Corps, which gave me a small monthly income.

"When I finished nurses' training in November of 1944, I went back home. A lot of my classmates went into the services. I went home to Long Island and entered the Army Nurse Corps at Fort Dix, New Jersey. I had been doing some teaching of nursing students during my final months at Medical College of Virginia. They sent me out to Fort Lewis, Washington, right near Seattle/Tacoma, to Madigan General Hospital. I was assigned to the Army Nurse Training Center as an instructor and Company Commander for new nurse recruits."

At Church with President Truman

"On Sunday, June 24, 1945, I was walking to the chapel to attend the church service at 11:00 am and saw more than the usual number of Military Police along the way. There were more near the chapel. I asked one of them why he was there at that time. He replied that President Truman was on his way to attend the church service. I felt honored to be there with the U.S. President!"

Overseas Orders, But Then the War Was Over

"Then I got overseas orders, heading to one of the islands or Japan. I went home for ten days and came back to Fort Lewis. But then the A-bomb came, and everything changed. So I never did go overseas. One of my roommates who had gone into the Army through Virginia was already over in the islands when the A-bomb came.

"It was sad that the bomb had to be used and that it killed so many people. However, it did end the war. If I had been sent for the invasion of Japan, I might not be here today. So I was really in the Army for only 18 months, mainly because toward the end of the war, overseas orders were discontinued."

Dorothy Managan, 1945, Ft. Lewis, Washington

Taking Care of Our Returning Prisoners of War

"I became the head of one of the wards for our own military personnel who had been prisoners of war. They were coming back on ships from Bataan, Corregidor, Burma, and China. I have a lot of written memories from these former POWs that they gave me. They were so happy to be back in the United States, and what they needed were hugs and a lot of tender loving care. They had a lot of different medical problems. Some amputees, some malnourished, some not able to use limbs, some with chronic diseases. They had lot of different problems they had not been getting any treatment for."

"The patients who had been prisoners of war were there at Fort Lewis until they were transferred back to Army hospitals closer to where they lived, where their family was. I have a lot of good memories of those times."

Following are some of those patients' affectionate and appreciative notes to Dorothy and the nursing staff, some teasing (that the nurses would miss the patients when they were gone).

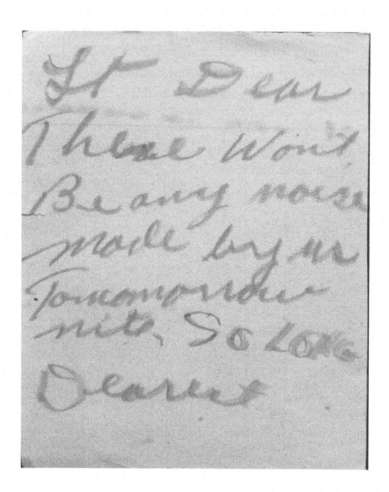

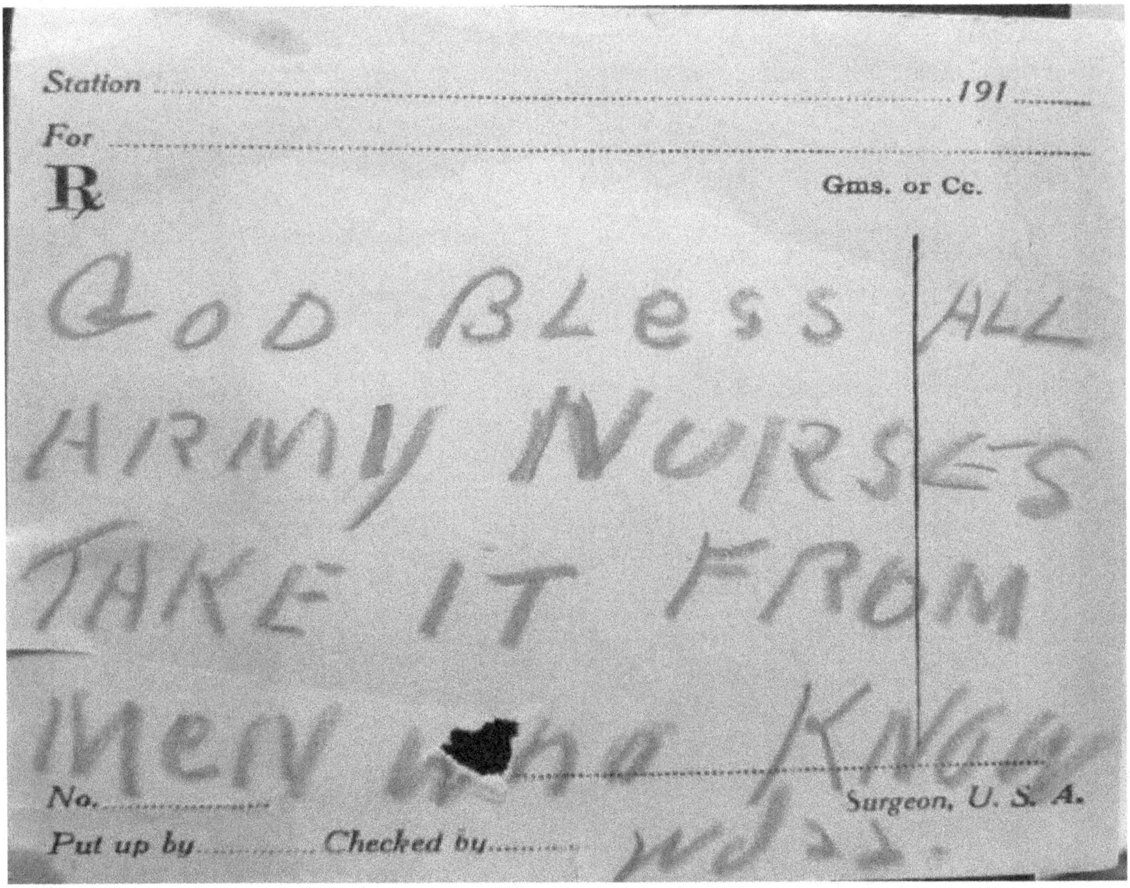

Station .... 191......

For ....

R   Gms. or Cc.

GOD BLESS ALL
ARMY NURSES
TAKE IT FROM
Men who KNOW.
WESS.

No. ....   Surgeon, U. S. A.

Put up by .... Checked by ....

NAME		GRADE	SERIAL No.
PART TO BE EXAMINED (OR TREATED)	HEART		
CLINICAL DIAGNOSIS (INCLUDE OPERATIONS) HEART BROKEN			
HOSPITAL MADIGAN Gen.	DATE Oct 30 1945		SIGNATURE Jahood

Broken Heart RESULTING
LOSING 56. WONDERFUL
PATIENTS.

Film No. XXXXX   Date Oct 30   Gen JAHOOD

WD AGO Form 8-63 1 December 1944
This form supersedes W. D., M. D. Form 55K-2, 9 June 1942,
which may be used until existing stocks are exhausted.   **RADIOLOGIC REPORT**

A patient has some fun with this "diagnosis" of the nurses

Training New Nurse Recruits

Back row, second from right: Dorothy Managan, nurse instructor, with new recruits

Below, training for gas attacks

Below, the students and instructors at Ft. Lewis, Washington

Relaxing. That's Dorothy indicated by the arrow.

Physical training—March!

Practice for setting a fracture and carrying the patient on a gurney

Poem to Dorothy (Tonjes at the time) and other instructors by nurse recruits:

IN TRIBUTE

Before we leave Fort Lewis,
And go on to our various posts,
We want to say "We're lucky
To have had you as hosts."

We came into the army
Not for glamour or for fun,
But because some soldier needs us,
And this battle must be won.

You have tried to make us soldiers,
Something strange to us, and new.
And we are so very grateful
To be helped by such a crew.

We have Maj. McKenzie, Jr.,
He's the finest in the land.
He's a soldier and a prince,
To us he's been just grand.

There is Lieutenant Anderson.
Goodness, but she's been swell.
Why she isn't now a Colonel
Only the army can tell.

Lieutenant Tonjes, our C.O.,
She's been a buddy true.
Like a sister and a mother,
She has seen our problems through.

Indeed, we are indebted,
To you and all the rest,
Who started us along our way,
You gave your very best.
We've really had a lot of fun,
And it wasn't bad at all.
We know that in the future,
It will be pleasant to recall.

And so to each and everyone,
Goes our sincerest "THANKS".
We hope we will still be worthy
To take our place in ranks.

"I mainly did my nursing duty during the end of the war and after the war was over, until June of 1946. Then I decided to ask for a discharge. I wanted to use the G.I. Bill to go back to school for my B.S. Degree. I was sent back to Fort Dix, N.J., and, along with two other nurses, hitchhiked back on a military plane. We left McCord Field on a B-17 and arrived at Lowery Field in Denver. Then we flew on a B-29 to Maryland with a stopover in Pittsburgh. I sat in the bombardier's seat.

Photos below are of the crew and of Dorothy and her friend.

After the War: Back to School

"I attended Western Reserve University in Cleveland, Ohio to get my baccalaureate degree. Later on I got a Master's in Public Health.

"While I was in school at Western Reserve, I attended the Church of the Covenant, right across the street from the school. They had a Sunday evening program for young adults, some of them just graduating from high school and others coming out of the service. I met the gentleman to be my future husband in that Sunday evening group called Tower Fellowship. We were married in July of 1948. I graduated with my baccalaureate degree in June of 1949.

"Then I was pregnant and in November I had my first child, a son. I have five children. I decided to get back into nursing, took a refresher course, and realized that, with a family, the hospital hours were not appropriate for family living. We were living in Wheaton, Illinois. My husband was working at Argonne National Lab. He had been in the Navy as a physicist. So I decided to get my Master's in Community Health at Northern Illinois University. The county health department had an excellent nursing division, so I went to work there doing home care and school visits. Then I became involved with a research project with the University of Illinois: 'Health Needs of Older Adults'. That's what led me into public health. I was working at the same time."

Retirement and Family

"Finally, in 1980, my husband and I both retired and we decided we were going to move Hendersonville. We had always loved camping, so we could camp in the mountains and we were only five hours from Myrtle Beach for camping. We were due to move down in 1983, but my husband died before we had a chance to move. We had friends in Hendersonville, so I decided to move down anyway. I live in Hendersonville still.

Dorothy's family of 41 gathered around her in Bar Harbor in 2016

"Our five children live all over the United States: Northeast Virginia, Rochester, N.Y., Bellingham, Washington, California, and Lexington, Kentucky. I now have 41 family members, including the daughters-in-law, sons-in-law, grandchildren and their spouses, and great-grandchildren. They drive me or fly me to their homes for frequent long stays. When we have family gatherings, everyone comes from all over the country to be together."

Dorothy Managan in 2019

Rufus "Pooch" Pace, Corporal, U.S. Army Air Corps and Sergeant, U.S. Air Force

Corporal Pooch Pace, Control Tower Operator, U.S. Army Air Corps, Kisarazu Air Base, Japan

Pooch Pace entered the U.S. Army Air Corps in 1945 at age 18, served in Japan after WWII, and in 1951 active duty in the U.S. Air Force Reserves in Texas during the Korean War. He was discharged 18 April, 1947, 1ˢᵗ enlistment.

Growing Up

During the Great Depression (in 1931) Pooch Pace was four years old. His family was living on the Greenville Highway, U.S. 25 South, in Hendersonville, North Carolina. Pooch recalls, "A lot of people were moving, trying to find work. Many families stopped [at our house] and asked if we had anything they could eat. A lot of the children would be crying because they were so hungry. Our mother would always help as she could. It was a very hard time for everyone.

"In 1932 we moved temporarily to Highway 191, Haywood Road, in preparation to move to a farm in Horse Shoe on Banner Farm Road. I started school at Mills River Grade School. In 1934 we moved to Marfin Farm. The name of the farm was from my parents, Margaret and Finley. The farm house was very old. There wasn't electricity and plumbing in the house and the water came from a hand-dug well. Lighting was kerosene lamps, cooking and heating was by wood stoves. The toilet was referred to as a two-holer. Bathing was in a tin tub. It was primitive living for a while, but we managed OK. Everything continued to progress and the farm was turned into dairying. There was always plenty of work to be done.

"I enlisted in the Army at the end of World War II and was sent to Fort Bragg, N.C., for the physical and aptitude test. Having some flight training and experience with maintaining a farm, I was assigned to the Army Air Corps and sent for training to Keesle Field, Mississippi. When I completed basic training, it was decided that aircraft mechanics were not needed, as fighting and bombing had stopped. Scoring a high rating in air identification and Morse Code, I was qualified to be trained as a control tower operator.

"Radio school at Scott Field, Illinois, was a great experience. Getting to go to Missouri's St. Louis Zoo was very thrilling. Langley Field, Virginia, was my next assignment for advanced training. Langley Field is headquarters for Army Airways Communication Services around the world, better known as A.A.C.S. During World War II, these operations were moved to Asheville, N.C., for security reasons.

"Completing training at Langley Field, we were told we would be going to Alaska. Our lightweight clothing was taken and heavier wool clothing and boots were issued. We arrived in Chicago, on July 1, 1946. Our train cars of 60 men were disconnected and switched to a siding [turnout]. We were told that a change in orders was being sent and that was the reason for our stopping. The officer in charge made arrangements with a tour company to pick us up and give a wonderful trip around Chicago. I was amazed at the vastness of the train switching rails, miles and miles. I have wondered if there is any other rail system that has a larger rail yard.

"On July 2nd, 1946, we were reconnected to a train headed for Seattle, Washington. We were told that we were headed to Japan and China. We traveled on a Victory Ship up by Alaska and the Aleutian Islands, but never close enough to see land. Several times we saw smaller fishing ships. Their catch would be carried to a large processing vessel. The trip was calm and restful."

Post-war Japan

"Upon arriving in Yokohama, Japan, some of the troops were staying aboard the ship, and they would be traveling to China. We were placed on a train and sent to the 4th Replacement Center. It was at night when we arrived. We asked about our supper and told them we hadn't eaten since our noon meal aboard ship. We were told the mess halls were closed and they had no way of feeding us. We were given a sleeping bag and folding cot and told what time breakfast would be served.

"The following morning we were processed and sent to Tokyo. Because of the large amount of troops arriving in Japan, sometimes finding adequate quarters became difficult. The building that the Army used to quarter the troops before assignment was full, so my group was sent to the living facilities under the stadium seating at the 1930 Tokyo Olympics. Everything I was seeing was a wonderful experience. I went in to where the swimming pool was. I had never seen a swimming pool that large. I finally dove in the pool off a 10-foot tower. I was trying to enjoy the excitement of seeing everything.

"We went to Johnson Field in Irumagawa, north of Tokyo. That was my first experience in a control tower. A control tower was being constructed. In those days they were built like the fire towers that protect our forests. While the control tower was being constructed, a van with a plastic bubble was being used.

"During the last week of July, 1946, I was assigned my first duty as a tower operator. The sergeant in charge said that a flight of four aircraft had gone to meet a gunner range for firing practice and would be calling in. The 1st flight was Tiny Red Flight, 2nd Tiny Blue Flight, 3rd Tiny Yellow Flight, 4th Tiny Green. The sergeant said he needed to be out of the control center for a few minutes and left. He asked if he could bring me anything to drink. My answer was no. I prayed to God that everything would be quiet.

"Everything was quiet for a few minutes. A photo-recon B-24 called in for taxi and take-off instructions. This went off smoothly. A few minutes later, Tiny Red Flight with 3 Chick called in requesting landing instructions. I cleared them into a right hand pattern for landing. I was informed that a straight-in approach was requested because overheating of engines of low-altitude flying. Straight-in approach was approved.

"Tiny Red Flight all made good landings. As Tiny Blue Flight approached, it was noted that aircraft #3 did not have its left landing gear down. Aircraft #3 was informed of this and was requested to pull up. Suddenly, all four planes of Tiny Blue Flight pulled up. Tiny Yellow and Tiny Green Flights made good, normal landings.

"Tiny Blue Flight #3 did a maneuver to get the landing gear locked down. Again, Tiny Blue Flight called in for landing instructions. Instructions granted. My first day as a control tower operator will never be forgotten!

"While the sergeant was in another mobile unit getting coffee, he could see what was happening. I like to scared him to death because he didn't know how I was going to respond my first time alone with that possible crash. When he came back he told me he had spilled coffee on himself, but I think he wet his pants," Pooch smiled. "That's what I always told him. That all happened within my first few minutes in a control tower. What an experience!

"I got to know a lot of the pilots of the B-24s we had there. They were flying all over Japan, China, and Korea with great big cameras doing photo recon [reconnaissance]. They were photographing everything from 10,000 feet. I got to hop rides and see Japan from the air—Hiroshima and Nagasaki. The fire from the bombs had annihilated everything. You could see the outlines of everything that fell—utility poles, people, everything.

"The Japanese munitions had been destroyed by the time I got there. They had taken all the guns and small munitions out and dumped them in Tokyo Bay. There had been big cannons all around the bay. Our Army had crammed something in the ends of the cannons and exploded them. Naturally, that ripped the barrels apart. Down in the bay, the Japanese had had pill boxes with soldiers in them. If we had invaded Japan, they were planning on blowing up our landing craft. That would have killed thousands or millions of people. I thank God that He let us have the atomic bomb. It saved many, many lives.

"And I was fortunate that I got in radio school when I did. I saw some of my friends crash and not survive, but it was from mechanical failures. My best friend, a P-51 Mustang pilot, crashed and didn't survive. I was in the tower at the time waiting for him. We had planned to go out together that afternoon. I got on the crash truck and went out to the crash. He was from Texas and wore cowboy boots. One of his boots had his kneecap in it. I had other friends get shot down over Czechoslovakia and Germany."

Japan's Kisarazu Air Base

"Then I was sent to Kisarazu Air Base. All the fighter planes that were coming into Japan came through there to be tested before going to Korea. We had 49 enlisted men and six officers—test pilots. Then they started bringing in jets.

Pooch Pace worked in the air control tower which is seen in the center of this photo.

"Kisarazu was where the Japanese had trained kamikaze pilots. The kamikaze planes didn't have landing gear. The pilots were trained to die. The little planes were carried up in the air by other large planes, which shot them out like a Roman candle. They were supposed to crash into our boats and, of course, blow up on impact. Before they sent the kamikaze pilots out on missions, they would let them smoke pot to relax. Because so many of them overdosed and died, they had built their own crematorium right there.

"After the war while I was there, they had an outbreak of cholera and so many died. They brought them there 24 hours a day to be cremated because they had to dispose of the decomposing bodies. They used a very poor fuel—gassified charcoal and peat moss. It looked like burning tires—the blackest, ropiest stuff you ever saw coming out of that chimney."

This is the first Jeep with a radio that was flown to Japan when the U.S. was planning to invade Japan. Pooch Pace sits in the Jeep wearing a microphone and headphone, at Kisarazu Air Base.

Pooch Pace (center) with other Control Tower Operators in their barracks on Kisarazu Air Base

Back Home in Hendersonville

Pooch came out of the Army in March of 1947, after his 18-month enlistment. He went to work for his father, who owned a heating and air conditioning business in Hendersonville. Pooch said, "I had promised my mother I would finish high school when I got out of service. When I left school, high school only went through the 11th grade. They had added another year while I was gone, so I had to finish the 11th and the 12th to graduate. I did it."

Country Boy Working at the FBI

"I had a buddy who lived in Washington, D.C., so I decided I'd go up there. I got a job with the fingerprinting division of the F.B.I. I didn't realize that Washington was such a party town. While I was there, President Truman was photographed falling while getting on his yacht for partying, and it was in the paper. The next day our boss came around and took my newspaper away so that picture wouldn't be seen.

"My friend and I got invitations from women who worked for congressmen to go with them to parties at the embassies as their escorts. In those days, we manually counted the lines on fingerprints to identify them. We had to look through a magnifying glass and count the number of whorls, loops, and deltas. But I soon found out that was pretty hard to do after a night of partying, and that was no place for a country boy. So I quit after three months and came home and worked as a mechanic for my father, who was in the heating and air conditioning business in Hendersonville."

Korean War Era: The Army Air Corps Is Now the U.S. Air Force

"I took some classes at Mars Hill College. When the Korean War started up in 1950, I was called up. By then the Air Force had been created as a separate branch of the military, so I was now in the Air Force, not the Army Air Corps. I wanted to go overseas, but they wouldn't let reservists go, so they sent me to Carswell Air Force Base, Fort Worth, Texas.

"I was sent to Perrin Air Force Base, Texas. They tried to get me to be a pilot, to fly transport planes. I had gotten my private pilot's license at Myers Flying Service in Hendersonville, N.C. I didn't do it. I told them I didn't want to be responsible for other people's lives. After that, they wouldn't even let me get in an airplane. So I requested release and came home in 1951."

Back Home in Hendersonville Again

"I came back here to live and continued in the heating and air conditioning business. I lost family and friends who were pilots. Do you know that out of 16 million men and women who served in World War II, only 800,000 are living now? There aren't many of us left. Now I help with military funerals. It's therapeutic; it helps me."

Pooch and his wife Jean live in Hendersonville They celebrated their 60th wedding anniversary in 2016.

322

Cornell Secosan, U.S. Navy

RM 3/C Cornell Secosan

Cornell Secosan joined the U.S. Navy in Cincinnati, in 1944, and served in the Pacific until mid-1946.

World War I Heritage

Cornell Secosan begins his military history by telling about his father's service in World War I. "My father came to America from Romania when he was 16. He had become an orphan when he was seven. At age nine, he was given a farm job in a neighboring village occupied by German-speaking people. He worked in the field with the men and slept in the barn with the animals.

"When he was 16, his brothers and sisters all chipped in to buy his one-way passage to the land of opportunity. He was alone and could speak no English. He could speak Romanian and German. He was about 29 when World War I started, living in Cincinnati. He went over to Fort Thomas, Kentucky, and volunteered for the Army. The Sergeant discouraged him from signing up. 'Well, you S.O.B., you go over there, you might shoot your cousins or brothers or somebody.' My father told him, 'You listen to me now, you S.O.B., you sign me up. I love this country. I make my living here. I'll fight for it.' So the Sergeant signed him up. My father told me, 'That's the last time I ever called a Sergeant an S.O.B.' His name was Bell Secosan. He became a Machine Gunner. He loved this country."

**Machine Gunner
Bell Secosan, World War I**

Engineering School and Joining the Navy

*"The Ole Dirty Bird"
USS Black Hawk (AD 9)*

Cornell begins his own story. "I was born and raised in Cincinnati, Ohio. I received a scholarship to the University of Cincinnati during my senior year in high school. So in June, 1944, I had completed one year of engineering at the University.

"I saw some of my friends going into service and I wanted to volunteer, but my father said, 'You finish your year at University of Cincinnati. They know where you live.' I registered for the draft on July 13, 1944. In October, 1944, I was at Great Lakes, Illinois, in the Navy. Then I went to radio school in Los Angeles, and to Camp Shumaker and San Francisco."

Deployment to Japan and China

"We went to Hawaii and got on *The U.S.S. Blackhawk*, a destroyer tender. A destroyer tender was like a floating machine shop. We could repair just about anything up to a five-inch bore on a destroyer.

"The war in the Pacific had ended. We went to Okinawa, Japan, a few weeks after the war ended. A typhoon was coming. We were ordered to leave by 5:00 on a certain day, but we had 200 sailors on shore at a beer and Coke party. The captain said, 'We're not leaving 200 men ashore, so he sent several masters with arms to find the men. They were all brought back. When the last man came aboard, the gangway was pulled up and we left. Three destroyers that didn't leave were lost."

Repatriation of Japanese Prisoners

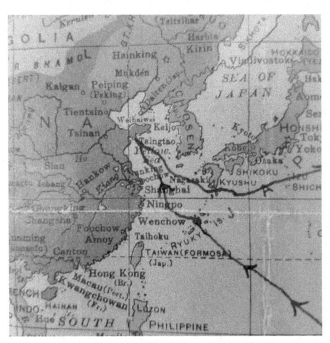

"We got orders to go to Tsingtao, China, with the Marines to repatriate the Japanese prisoners who were in China. The prisoners were moved from Tsingtao to Shanghai, then to Japan.

"We were there to support the movement of those prisoners back to Japan. Our ship was there to make repairs to the ships in that area."

At right, Japanese
prisoners being moved
by Marines from
China back to Japan

"I was a Radio Operator. The Navy sent out encoded messages 24 hours a day. The messages were about ship movement."

From left, Cornell's friend
"Black Dog," and "Seco"
(Cornell) Secosan

326

Scenes in Tsingtao, China, during the repatriation of the Japanese prisoners in 1945

In his photo album, Cornell had labeled this photo (top) "Curious Children." On the street in Tsingtao, they gathered around the sailors. He explained, "They were curious whether we were going to give them candy bars or cigarettes. We did." (below)

A Japanese bayonet Cornell picked up on the ground
on Okinawa

Cornell took this photo of his buddy Bob at a temple in
Tsingtao, China.

"We were in Tsingtao on Christmas Eve, 1945. I was on duty till midnight. When I went topside I saw all the Navy ships with their lights strung for Christmas. That was the only time I was ever homesick."

Going Home

"We came back to San Francisco in May of '46.

Right "Homeward Bound" pennant flying (in center of photo), a welcome sight for sailors on their way home.

Homeward Bound Pennant Flying

Below, a close-up of the "Homeward Bound" pennant, showing signatures of

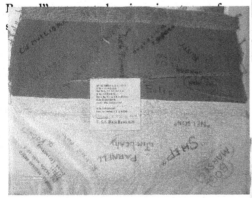

At right, the history of voyages by the U.S.S. Blackhawk. This label is also seen in the center of the pennant above.

Left San Francisco U. S. A. 5-21-45
At Sea 5- 21- 45:5-31-45
Pearl Harbor T.H. 5-31-45:9-11-45
At Sea 9-11-45:9-30-45
Buckner Bay, Okinawa 9-30-45:11-30-45
At Sea 11-30-45:12-4-45
Tsingtao, China 12-4-45:5-20-46

At Sea 5-20-46:6-12-46
Arrive, San Francisco, U. S. A. 6-12-46

CORNELL SECOBAN RM3/

U. S. S. Black Hawk AD9

"I was discharged on May 12, 1946. I arrived home at 7:30 A.M. on my 20th birthday, after traveling all night from Great Lakes to Cincinnati. My mother made me a wonderful breakfast of bacon, eggs, and toast. I picked up the toast and held it up to the light. Mother said, 'What are you doing?' I told her it was a habit we had on the ship. Often our bread had bugs in it, because the flour was old from many days at sea. We'd pick out the bugs and eat the bread."

Cornell's first day home from the Pacific on his 20th birthday

Sailors' mothers would buy flags to hang in their windows to show that their son or daughter was serving in the Navy. This one hung in Cornell's parents' home.

After he was discharged from the Navy in 1946, Cornell went back to the University of Cincinnati and completed his five-year engineering degree. He went to work for Procter & Gamble, where he ran manufacturing operations making Crisco, margarine, peanut butter, and other products. He traveled all over the world for Procter & Gamble as manager of the international manufacturing staff department. His career with P&G spanned 37 years.

After retirement, Cornell and his wife Dorothy moved to Brevard in 1990 to be near his son, daughter-in-law, and grandchildren. He is shown here in his Connestee Falls home in 2016.

He and his wife volunteered as tutors to first-graders at Pisgah Forest Elementary School for 22 years. One of his favorite things to teach the first-graders was about America's fighting of the wars which gives us our freedoms and way of life.

Each Veterans' Day, Cornell gave a VFW poppy to every first grader. Then he told the children about Flanders Field and his father's service during World War I, as well as his own service in World War II. Cornell explained that sometimes America must fight in order to preserve our freedoms and way of life.

He always ended his lesson with a quote from General Douglas MacArthur, who accepted the Japanese surrender. MacArthur's farewell address to West Point Academy in 1961 was titled 'Honor, Duty, Country.' He explained to the first-graders that "Your responsibility is to honor your parents, teachers, other students, and yourselves. Your duty is to do the best you can at school. And you should always remember that even though this country isn't perfect, it's the best anybody's come up with."

"I get teed off when people say negative things about America," Cornell said. "We are very, very lucky to have been born in this country."

Cornell's dog tags, key to his locker aboard *The Blackhawk,* and the medals awarded to him

Col. Charles William "Bill" Tierney (Ret.), U.S. Army Reserves and PFC, U.S. Marine Corps

PFC Bill Tierney, 1945, U.S.M.C.

Bill Tierney was drafted into the Marines in 1945, in Lima, Ohio.
He served in the Pacific in WWII, and later in the Korean War. He served in the reserves for 36 years.

Deployed to Invade Japan, but . . .

When 18-year-old Bill Tierney and 8,000 Marines boarded the attack transport *The Wakefield** in Norfolk, Virginia, in 1945, they sailed through the Panama Canal and headed for Pearl Harbor. They were expecting to mount an attack on mainland Japan. Upon arrival at Pearl, they were told that the atom bombs had been dropped on Hiroshima and Nagasaki, and that the war was over. "Thank God," Bill said. "That saved all of our lives."

U.S.S. Wakefield (later photo), which was a converted ocean liner (*The Manhattan*)

"I remember on Pearl Harbor, the bugle sounded "To the Colors" and we were called to attention. All the Marines came to attention immediately. That's what a Marine would do. There were some Navy sailors puddling around in the swimming pool that was beside the slop chute (bar), and they just stayed where they were. The Navy kept right on swimming. We Marines just stood and watched them. The old Marine just let go of his beer can and said, 'Come out of there, you dumb S.O.B.s. To the Colors!' That was when the fight almost started. The Colonel in charge said, 'You want to fight? I can arrange that.' We all backed off and went our separate ways without a fight. I'll never forget that."

Relocated to Fight in China

"So then we, E Company, 2nd Battalion, 1st Division, 7th Marines, were deployed to make the main assault on China to fight Mao's communist troops. They were sending all the remaining Japanese back to Japan. In Tientsin in Northern China, we were tied in with the Chinese Nationalists. Our barbed wire tied in with theirs.

"We moved into the outpost line in Shi-lung, in northern China. We went to battle stations. I was on a ridge looking down a creek line. I have a crease on my head

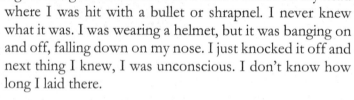

where I was hit with a bullet or shrapnel. I never knew what it was. I was wearing a helmet, but it was banging on and off, falling down on my nose. I just knocked it off and next thing I knew, I was unconscious. I don't know how long I laid there.

"The corpsman came and checked me out and said, 'You're all right. You got hit but it's not serious.' I had a sore head, but I got up and went back to the fight. We were all just kids."

With a chuckle, Bill told this story: "Seven Marines left their post and took their beer to an ice house to ice their beer up. The Communists grabbed them right off the bat. We heard that they had been taken off toward the ocean. The old man (our commander) called us together and told us to go after them. So we chased them on foot for a couple of days. Finally they either got tired of us chasing them or they were afraid we might chew 'em up when we caught them. So we got our guys back. The old man probably locked 'em up.

"Every once in a while the Communists would snipe at us and we'd say, 'Well, that's life,' and keep down and out of sight. I turned 19 years old while I was in China. We were tasked to protect the coal supply as the train traveled from the coal mine to the cities. Four-man teams would protect the coal—one on the engine and three on the caboose.

"Here's a picture of a little Chinese boy, naked in the winter. He and his mother were picking up pieces of coal that fell off the train car. They were poor and needed fuel to keep warm. I was guarding the caboose, I looked out the window and saw this little boy. Someone took a picture of me handing him some C-rations for himself and his mother to eat."

Active Duty in Korea

Bill Tierney had been drafted into the Marines in 1945 within one week of his graduation from St. Gerard High School in Lima, Ohio. "But after almost two years in the Corps, when I came back from China," he said, "I was tossed out. The Marines did not want younger guys my age.

"A bunch of us who liked the military joined the Army National Guard. I was called up to active duty in 1953 and went to Korea. It was near the end of the war. The Old Man decided that I should be an officer. I wasn't exactly in the fighting, but I knew and saw a lot of things.

"Korea was nasty. We had heavy casualties. I was there for about a year. I was there when the war ended. I saw the exchange of prisoners when our boys came back. Helicopters were picking them up and taking them to the hospitals. Our flights home were canceled so the P.O.W.s could be transported home first."

Service Back in the States

"When I came back to Ohio, I stayed in the Reserves. I enjoyed it. I had good people. I commanded small units. As time went by, I got better and better jobs and was commissioned a full colonel. I went to work for the Nickel Plate Railroad, which became Western Railroad, then became Norfolk Southern Railroad. All my family had worked for railroads. I started out on steam trains. I was a conductor.

"Several times I asked for a leave of absence and went back on active duty. I taught reservists for the Army at Fort Bragg, N.C. I taught Aerial Imagery Interpretation and Aerial Surveillance. I loved teaching. People say I was a ham. One morning I had an early class. Students started filtering in and the next thing I know I've got 100 students. I thought, 'How will I get through this?'

"I had two students in every seat. I got through it. I've always been a people person, so I just got on the stage and talked to them as if I was talking to each individual. Eventually I became commander of the school at Ft .Bragg, and was in the Reserves for 36 years.

"I volunteered for Vietnam, but my son was already there, so they wouldn't send me. My son came home OK, and I was tickled to death. Part of my time was  wonderful and I enjoyed it." Asked what parts he enjoyed, he said, "The responsibility. You have a mission. You do it. Then you look up and ask yourself, 'How did I do?' and if you did it well, you recognize it. But we took some awful casualties. I was lucky. I'm just glad it's over."

Bill and his wife Jenny (at left) moved to Brevard in 2003.

**Ret. Colonel C.W. Bill Tierney,
Nov. 4, 2016**

EPILOGUE

Many of the veterans who gave me their stories downplayed the importance of their roles in the war. Some said, "I wasn't a hero", or "My story isn't a glorious one". Some felt guilty that they came home from the war while their buddies didn't.

All our veterans, whether they "saw action" or not, played vital roles to help us win the war. They all trained, prepared, and sacrificed time from their loved ones to be ready. Others supported the fighting troops with vital services that made everything else work. It took everyone to create the victory which saved our freedom, liberty, and our way of life.

People at home also worked to support the war. My mother worked in a cotton mill that made the yarn for t-shirts for the U.S. Navy. My aunt worked in a shipyard as a "Rosie the Riveter". Whole industries retooled to make war materiel. Automobile factories produced aircraft. Washing machine factories made machine guns.

Together, our brave, selfless service members and the people at home saved Western Civilization for us. We thank you. Collecting your stories for this book is my way of honoring you for what you did for us.

Janis Allen
January 2, 2017

"WE SHALL COME HOME VICTORIOUS."

HONOR · EDUCATE · PRESERVE
Remembering and Honoring our Veterans

Veterans History Museum of the Carolinas
Brevard, North Carolina, U.S.A.
www.theveteransmuseum.org
emmett@theveteransmuseum.org

Honor, Educate, Preserve

The purpose of this museum is to provide an avenue for people to appreciate and honor the men and women who served so bravely in our Armed Forces.

The museum displays one-of-a-kind artifacts, uniforms, weaponry, original newspapers, personal letters, etc. All of these special items weave the great and proud stories of World

War I, World War II, Korea, The Cold War, Vietnam, Iraq, and Afghanistan.

These displays help us empathize with the wonder, but also the danger, of our involvement in these wars, and the unique sacrifice of our military men and women!

The museum demonstrates love of country and gratitude to those who serve and have served.

BOOKS BY JANIS ALLEN

PERFORMANCE TEAMS: CREATING THE FEEDBACK LOOP

I SAW WHAT YOU DID AND I KNOW WHO YOU ARE (WITH GAIL SNYDER)

TEAM UP!

YOU MADE MY DAY: CREATING CO-WORKER RECOGNITION AND
RELATIONSHIPS (WITH MICHAEL MCCARTHY)

STORIES FROM A SANDY MUSH GIRL

HOW TO ENGAGE, INVOLVE, AND MOTIVATE EMPLOYEES
(WITH MICHAEL MCCARTHY)

READY? SET? ENGAGE!
(WITH MICHAEL MCCARTHY)

FROM BOO-HISS TO BRAVO:
BEHAVIOR-BASED SCORECARDS PEOPLE WILL USE AND LIKE

Made in USA - North Chelmsford, MA
1166360_9798639968655
10.12.2021 1024